THE CATHOLIC UNIVERSITY OF AMERICA
CANON LAW STUDIES
Number 64

THE BANNS OF MARRIAGE

AN HISTORICAL SYNOPSIS AND COMMENTARY

A DISSERTATION

Submitted to the Faculty of Canon Law of the Catholic University of America in Partial Fulfillment of the Requirements for the Degree of

DOCTOR OF CANON LAW

BY THE

REVEREND JAMES B. ROBERTS, A.B., J.C.L.
Priest of the Archdiocese of New York

THE CATHOLIC UNIVERSITY OF AMERICA
WASHINGTON, D. C.
1931

Nihil Obstat:

VALENTINUS T. SCHAAF, O.F.M., J.C.D.,
Censor Deputatus.

Washingtonii, D. C., die xxiii Aprilis, 1931.

Imprimatur:

PATRITIUS CARDINALIS HAYES,
Archiepiscopus Neo Eboracensis.

NEO EBORACI, DIE IV MAII, 1931.

WASHINGTON TYPOGRAPHERS, INC.
WASHINGTON, D. C.

TABLE OF CONTENTS

FOREWORD

For seven centuries and more, Sunday after Sunday, pastors have been publishing the banns of marriage. Of all the weddings they have announced, comparatively few have met with any opposition or accusation. Yet the Church has retained the legislation, and insisted time and again on its observance. The publicity resulting from the banns was not an end in itself, nor were clandestine marriages forbidden merely because of their secret character. They were outlawed because of the evils which, experience proved, so often accompanied them.

Long before the institution of the banns, from the very beginning of her history, the Church has devoted every effort to root out the abuse. The canonical legislation as it now exists wields a threefold check on clandestinity—the investigation by the pastor regarding the free state of the parties; the publication of the banns; and the enforcement of the observance of a juridical form in the celebration of marriage. Each represents a stage in the development of the law, and each acts as a supplement to the other.

The canonical concept of "clandestinity" has varied somewhat in the different periods. The older canonists included under it the impediment of age, the lack of parental consent, and the violation of *sponsalia*.[1] After the Fourth Lateran Council, three species of clandestinity were generally recognized: that arising from the secret contracting of marriage, that springing from the omission of the liturgical rites of the marriage ceremony, and that caused by the failure to publish the banns.[2] Since the introduction of the canonical form by the Council of Trent, the term is generally applied to those marriages entered

[1] Thus, Soto, *Comment. in IV Sent.*, D. 28, q. 1, a. 1.

[2] Soto, *Comment, in IV Sent.*, D. 28, q. 1, a. 1; Bernardus Papiensis, *Summa*, IV, 141; Constitution of Bourges, 1263, n. v.,—Harduin, VII, 554; Feije, *De Imped. et Disp.*, I, 242; Esmein, *Le Mariage en Droit Canonique*, (2 ed.), I, 205.

into without the presence of the pastor, or other duly authorized priest, and the two witnesses.[3] Nevertheless, authors continue to use it in a certain wider sense to designate bannless marriages also.[4]

The principal purpose of the banns is to forestall invalid marriages by the discovery of latent impediments. The Church found that the personal examination conducted by the pastor was not always successful, and she therefore introduced the banns, in order to enlist the aid of all in carrying out this investigation. However, the banns serve other very important functions. Their publication must ordinarily extend over a period of two or three weeks. In that interval at least, the parties are given time for reflection on the serious character of the marriage contract, and are deterred from entering into it hastily and without due consideration of its difficulties. This delay also gives the priest an opportunity to instruct the couple properly, and to prepare them for the worthy reception of the Sacrament of Matrimony.

So much of the matrimonial legislation has been given irritating or inhabilitating force, that the remainder oftentimes seems to suffer by comparison. The distinction between the two types of law is exaggerated to the point of making the preceptive regulations—the banns in particular—appear almost unimportant. This is a natural and unintentional reaction to the stress laid on the invalidating laws, and to avoid the fault, it is necessary to recall the value of the other canons. With this in mind, the writer proposes to discuss in this dissertation the legislation on the Banns of Marriage in its present form, and summarily in its historical background. Research work in the

---

[3] S. C. C., *Syracusen.*, 1587,—Pallottini, *Collectio Resol. S. C. C.*, XII, 532; S. C. C., *Neapolit.*, 14 Jun. 1884, ad 1,—*A. S.*, XVII [1884], 312; Wernz, *Jus Decretalium*, IV, 182.

[4] Barbosa, *Collectanea Doctorum*, 573; Sanchez, *De Matrimonio*, III, d. 1, nn. 7-9; Gutierrez, *Canon. Quest., de mat.*, c. lxxi, n. 9; D'Annibale, *Summula Theologiae Moralis*, III, n. 453; Wernz, *Jus Decretalium*, IV, 182. Cosci went so far as to say that a bannless marriage is the only kind of clandestine marriage. (*De Sponsalibus Vota Decisiva*, votum X, n. 18). The term "bannless marriages" is coined for convenience. It will be used to designate those cases in which the banns are culpably omitted.

history of the law was greatly hampered by the lack of sources.

The writer wishes to take this occasion to give public expression of his gratitude to the members of the Faculty of the School of Canon Law, to the Reverend Joseph MacCarthy, to the Reverend Avitus E. Lyons, and to the Reverend John J. McClafferty, for many favors.

PRELIMINARY DISCUSSION

Matrimonial Publication in Pre-Christian Legislation

The institution known as the banns of marriage is the proper theme of this dissertation. Yet it cannot be correctly appreciated if studied as an isolated experiment in human law. Like every other legal device, it must be examined on the background of its true and its analogous precedents. The history of matrimonial publication necessarily leads to a discussion of the juridical solemnities—the forms—of betrothment and marriage.[1] These forms will be treated briefly, and not in so much as they affect the validity or liceity of the marriage contract, but in their functions as means of attracting pubic notice to the celebration of the nuptials.

There were theologians who maintained that the natural law itself forbade clandestine marriage.[2] The more common opinion held and still holds to the contrary—namely, that the natural law does not forbid such marriages, but that human legislators and custom outlawed them under the guidance and dictates of natural reason.[3]

Throughout history, Christian and pagan, attempts have been made to abolish clandestine marriage. "Clandestine marriages, as they are productive of many evils in society, have always been discountenanced in well constituted governments; and have always been deemed more detrimental to the peace and good order of a nation, in proportion as it has been more civilized."[4]

---

[1] Wernz-Vidal, *Jus Canonicum,* V, n. 524: "Solemnitates in matrimonio contrahendo ex jure Ecclesiae adhibendae recte dicuntur matrimonii forma." Form is either juridical or liturgical. The juridical form is subdivided into substantial (that required for the validity of the contract), and accidental (that required for the lawful initiation of the contract).

[2] Sanchez, *De Matrimonio,* III, d. 3, n. 8.

[3] Schmalzgrueber, *Jus Ecclesiasticum,* IV, iii, nn. 93-94.

[4] Gally, *Considerations on Clandestine Marriage,* p. 1. Cfr. also, Westermarck, *History of Human Marriage,* p. 418; and Cook, in *Atlantic Monthly,* LXVIII [1888], 686.

It must be observed, however, that in most of the older legislations the ceremonial rites were optional, and were observed through custom rather than under the force or suggestion of written law.

It is difficult to determine with accuracy the practice obtaining in the very ancient civilizations. From the fragmentary extant records it has been established that weddings among the ancient Babylonians were accompanied with some sort of ritual and publicity. Its exact character has not been determined, but it is clear that certain officials were called upon to assist; who they were or what the ritual observances were is unknown.[5] The Athenians celebrated marriages solemnly, with a banquet, and amidst a large gathering of relatives and friends. Besides being a religious festival, this was designed to make public the marriage.[6]

Under Hebraic law espousal and marriage were entered into with a rather elaborate ceremonial, some traces of which may be found in Sacred Scripture itself. Westermarck denies that there was any religious element in these celebrations, but even apart from the question of the truth or falsity of this assertion, it must be admitted that they acted as a very effective check on clandestinity.[7] The first step was the betrothal. The prospective husband (or his father) made payment of the *mohar* (dowry price) to the girl's father, and entered into a written contract.[8] This engagement usually took place in the presence of witnesses, about a year before the marriage, or the consummation of the marriage.[9] On the day appointed for the wedding, the bride, "adorned with her jewels," was led in procession to the house of the bridegroom. The ceremony took place there in the presence of the rabbi and guests, amidst feasting and rejoicing.[10]

---

[5] Johns, *Babylonian and Assyrian Laws,* p. 132.

[6] Potter, *Greek Antiquities,* II, 288.

[7] Westermarck, *History of Human Marriage,* p. 425.

[8] There is a reference to this dowry arrangement in Genesis XXXIV, 12 and in I Kings, XVIII, 25. Cfr. Serrier, *Le Mariage Contrat-Sacrement,* p. 11: Brown, *Antiquities of the Jews,* II, 138.

[9] Brown, *loc. cit.,* holds that the time varied from one month to several years.

[10] The Scriptures afford a familiar instance of such a celebration at Cana

The Book of Ruth gives an example of a less solemn form—used perhaps because Ruth was a widow—but one which manifests the care taken to insure the public recognition of the marriage. "And Booz taking ten men of the ancients of the city, said to them: Sit ye down here. . . . And he said to the ancients and to all the people: You are witnesses this day, that I . . . have taken to wife Ruth the Moabitess. . . ."[11]

The most highly developed of the pre-Christian marriage codes was that of the Roman state. On many points ecclesiastical law bears the clear vestiges of this earlier legislation. Nevertheless, the Roman system, judged in the light of canon law, labored under a peculiar handicap—it was continually struggling between two opposed principles—wishing to leave matrimony a purely ethical institution, free from the fetters of juridical formality, and yet forced, because of the consequences of marriage, to enact certain restrictions.

In preventing unlawful unions, law can adopt two courses. It can establish a complete ante-nuptial investigation of the status of both parties, which would render remote the possibility of marriage between those laboring under an impediment; or it can introduce such drastic penalties for those entering prohibited marriages, that subjects would prefer to avoid violating the law. Roman jurisprudence emphasized the latter mode of procedure, though it did not entirely neglect that of pre-nuptial publicity and wedding solemnities.

It is quite true that in all Roman law there is no institution even remotely resembling the banns of marriage, but there were adequate methods of achieving the ends served by the banns. The Romans clung tenaciously to the principle that consent was the constitutive element in marriage. In proving the existence of marriage, and differentiating it from concubinage, it was of primary importance to establish the fact that matrimonial intent was present from the beginning. Certain forms—taking that

---

of Galilee (John, II, 1-11). Brown, *Antiquities of the Jews,* II, 141; Serrier, *Le Mariage Contrat-Sacrement,* p. 12: "Le délai écoulé, le mariage est célebré au milieu des festins et de réjouissances: il se réduit au point de vue religieux, à quelques bénédictions et cérémonies symboliques."

[11] Ruth, IV, 2, 9 and 10.

word in its wide sense—were recognized as indicative of matrimonial consent. These may be placed under three headings: the ceremonies of *manus,* the arrangements preparatory to marriage, namely, *sponsalia* and dowry; and the *deductio in domum,* with the accompanying nuptial rites. What is said here with regard to these solemnities can be applied in its entirety only to those marriages which the Roman law considered as *nuptiae justae,* that is, valid marriage between two parties enjoying the *jus connubii,* a franchise practically restricted to Roman citizens. Other marriages were, to the Romans, *nuptiae non justae*—outside the consideration of the law, though in no way opposed to it.

During the post-classical and the Justinian periods, some efforts were made to establish a system of marriage registration.

There was a general ordinance promulgated by Theodosius and Valentius in 428, and reproduced by Justinian,[12] which required as a minimum of formality that the giving of matrimonial consent be known to the friends of the parties. Justinian made a law that obliged those in the higher professions to appear before the clergy, so that an official record of the marriage might be made.[13]

In none of these legal systems can there be found a true counterpart of the canonical pre-nuptial investigation and publication. They do offer evidence of the efforts of these ancient peoples to guard the sanctity of marriage, and they serve to accentuate by comparison the efficacy and value of the canonical legislation on these points.

---

[12] *Theod. Code,* III, 7, 3; *C.,* V, 4, 22. Gothofredus, commenting on the edict, says: " . . . sufficit aequalibus personis conveniens electio atque consensus, sic tamen ut conscientia intercedat amicorum."

[13] *Novellae,* LXXIV, 4, 2.

PART I

THE HISTORY OF MATRIMONIAL PUBLICATION IN CANON LAW

CHAPTER I

BEFORE THE INTRODUCTION OF THE BANNS

Christianity introduced a new and higher concept of matrimony—marriage as a Sacrament, deserving of reverence, not only in its own natural right, but as an instrument of divine grace as well. The union of man and wife was likened to that of Christ and His Church, and became recognized as a sacred state and office, through which were begotten the citizens of this world and the Saints of the next.

ART. 1. THE INVESTIGATION BY THE BISHOP

Though the Church has always regarded marriage as a matter of public interest,[1] she has not at all times employed the same vehicles of publicity. The banns were only a later development. In the early ages of the Faith, Christians were accustomed to consult the Bishop before entering marriage, and to submit to his advice and guidance.[2] This practice, introduced by custom, was intended to discourage marriage with infidels, as well as to safeguard the faithful from incestuous and otherwise prohibited unions. The simplicity of such a method of pre-nuptial investigation was quite in harmony with existing conditions. A more detailed inquiry, necessary in later centuries, was not needed then, first because the impediments of canon law were not so precisely determined, and also because the social structure of the Church was not so complex. Parishes were unheard of at that time, and the Bishop himself attended to many of the duties which have since devolved on pastors.

---

[1] Tertullian, *Liber de Pudicitia,* c. 4—*M. P. L.*, II, 987: "Ideo penes nos occultae quoque conjunctiones id est non prius apud Ecclesiam professae, juxta moechiam et fornicationem judicari periclitantur." Cfr. Bingham, *Christian Antiquities,* II, 1204.

[2] St. Ignatius, *Letter to Polycarp,* c. 5—*M. P. G.*, V, 723: "Decet vero, ut sponsi et sponsae de sententia episcopi conjugium faciant, ut nuptiae secundum Deum sint, non secundum cupiditatem."

Art. 2. Insistence on the Liturgical Ceremonies of Marriage

When the parochial system did come into existence, about the fifth century, the care of marriage arrangements was transferred to the pastors. In the writings of that period numerous references were made to the public solemnization of nuptials. Perhaps the insistence on the point by the Fathers of that age was due to a diminution of the fervor of the Christians, some of whom were disposed to disregard the custom of obtaining the sacerdotal blessing.[3] At Milan it was evidently the practice for the priest to impose the veil upon the bride, and give her his blessing.[4] The same rule prevailed in the Church at Rome, and in the African provinces.[5] No reference was made in these early ecclesiastical writings to any parochial investigation into the free state and hability of the parties. The stress was laid upon the public religious celebration of the marriage. This fact is probably explained by the large influx of converts from paganism, after the persecutions. It was necessary to impress upon these people the higher Christian ideals of marriage and its religious character.

There are also two very clear allusions to the publicity required, even during this early period, in celebrating marriage. St. Jerome, in his commentary on the fifth chapter of the Book of Proverbs, the sixth verse, says:[6] *In plateis tuis aquas tuas divide. Id est, filium tuum ac filiam aliis nuptui trade, et hoc manifeste cum pluribus sociis.* The other reference may be found in the fifteenth canon of the Council held at Verno in 755:[7] . . . *ut omnes homines laici publicam nuptiam faciant, tam nobiles, quam ignobiles.*

---

[3] Bingham, *Christian Antiquities*, II, 1222.

[4] St. Ambrose, *Letter to Vigilius*, c. 7—*M. P. L.*, XVI, 984.

[5] Innocent I, *Letter to Victor, Bishop of Rouen*, c. 6—*M. P. L.*, XX, 475; Siricius, *Letter to Himerius*, c. 4—*M. P. L.*, XIII, 1136; Canon XIII of the *Statuta Antiqua* ascribed to the IV Council of Carthage. Hefele, *Conciliengeschichte*, II, 71 gives the date of the council as 398, but notes that it is not certain that the council issued these laws, and it is his belief that these statutes are of later origin.

[6] *M. P. L.*, XXV, 402.

[7] Mansi, XII, 583; Hefele, *Conciliengeschichte*, III, 587.

Art. 3. The Parochial Investigation

About the end of the eighth century, councils began to enjoin upon the pastors the obligation of assuring themselves of the absence of all impediments to the marriage, by conducting a pre-nuptial investigation. The new element in the legal texts accompanied the development of the legislation on the impediments.[8] The Council of Friuli introduced in its eighth canon a regulation which resembled that of the Fourth Lateran Council, in all but demanding the banns. After the sponsalial agreement there was to be a definite interval during which the relatives and neighbors of the parties might be consulted, especially with regard to consanguinity. Those who failed to observe this rule and married secretly became liable to severe penalties if the marriage subsequently proved invalid.[9]

The councils of this period emphasized the impediments of consanguinity and affinity. The reason for this was that in those days both impediments were very frequently encountered; the forbidden degrees extended farther than they do at present, while the social intercourse of the people was practically limited to their own isolated neighborhoods.

The evil of clandestine marriage did not escape the vigilance of Charlemagne, who took it upon himself to outlaw it.[10] His statute specified that a diligent inquiry by the clergy and *seniores populi* was to precede the marriage and that it was to be contracted before a priest, and with the blessing of that priest.

The imperial decree met with no greater success than its ecclesiastical predecessors, for during the succeeding centuries councils and canonists found it necessary to devise means of combating secret marriage. In some instances, the investigation before marriage was explicitly insisted upon,[11] whereas others

---

[8] Carriere, *Praelectiones Theologicae,* III, #377.

[9] Conc. of Friuli, 791, c. 8—Mansi, XIII, 848.

[10] Capitulary of Charlemagne, A. D. 802, c. xxxv—*M. G. H.,* Leges, I, 98. A similar prescription is ascribed to the Synod of Ratisbon, 799, but it is not entirely certain that this canon is authentic—Hefele, *Conciliengeschichte,* III, 375.

[11] Benedictus Levita, *Capitularium Collectio,* III, n. 179—*M. P. L.,*

were satisfied with demanding the public celebration of the marriage.[12] The investigation outlined in the Capitulary of Benedictus Levita, as cited above, must have been in reality a publication of the proposed marriage, similar to the banns; it was to be conducted by the priest, not through private inquiry, but publicly in the church, where he was to question the people there assembled as to whether they knew of any obstacle to the marriage— . . . *in ecclesia coram populo. Et ibi inquirere una cum populo ipse sacerdos debet. . . .*

Legislators sometimes regulated by statute the ceremonies to be observed. The most prominent of these ordinances was the decree of Pope Nicholas I.[13] Great missionary activity was in progress in Bulgaria at the time, and the ruler, Prince Boris, consulted Pope Nicholas on several questions, including this one about the celebration of marriage. The Pope outlined the practice observed at Rome.[14] In his letters, the Pope declared that marriage should be preceded by betrothal, that a dowry should be arranged, and the consent of the parents obtained. The wedding itself was to be publicly celebrated in the church, the parties receiving the priestly blessing. Duschesne[15] traces these solemnities to the ceremonies of pre-Christian Rome. Practically the same formula seems to have been in use in France, at about the same time.[16]

XCVII, 820. (Whatever the origin and authenticity of this collection, it serves as a witness to the then existing conditions.) Another reference to this pre-nuptial investigation may be found in the acts of the Council of Rouen, 1072, c. xiv—Mansi, XX, 38.

[12] Peter Damien, *De Tempore Celebrandi Nuptias*, c. iii—*M. P. L.*, CXLV, 663; Yves of Chartres, *De Conjugiis*, part 8—*M. P. L.*, CLXI, 853; Hugh of St. Victor, *De Sacramentis*, II, part 2, c. 6—*M. P. L.*, CLXXVI, 448.

[13] *Decreta Nicolai Papae I*, t. xviii, n. 4—Mansi, XV, 446.

[14] *Responsa ad Bulgarum Consulta*, 866, c. iii, *de sponsis*,—Mansi, XV, 402: " . . . morem, quem sancta Romana antiquitus, et hactenus in hujusmodi conjunctionibus tenet ecclesia . . . "

[15] *Christian Worship*, p. 413.

[16] Council of Trosly, 909, c. viii—Mansi, XVIII, A, 287; Council of Rouen, 1072, c. xiii—Mansi, XX, 38 and Martène, *De Antiquis Eccles. Ritibus*, I, part 2, 604. To this period can be ascribed also the pseudo-Isidorean *Decreta Evaristi Papae*, c. *de conjugio legitimo*,—*M. P. L.*, CXXX, 81.

Art. 4. Marriage "in facie Ecclesiae"

The Germanic nations retained many of their old customs after their conversion, and among these their nuptial solemnities. Because these practices served to guarantee the publicity of marriage, the Popes encouraged the observance of them. It was the custom with these peoples to celebrate the marriage publicly at the doors of the church—literally, *in conspectu* or *in facie Ecclesiae.* The practice was soon adopted in other parts of Europe.[17]

Art. 5. Celebration of Marriage in the Presence of Witnesses

Two other enactments against clandestine marriage merit special mention, because they introduced a new note into the ecclesiastical legislation. Besides prescribing general publicity, they ordained that marriage was to be celebrated in the presence of certain determined witnesses.[18] In that way, the fact of marriage could be juridically established more easily. Why the provisions of these two decrees did not engage more widespread attention at the time is impossible to say.

In the writings of several of the authors lengthy treatises were devoted to a consideration and condemnation of secret marriage.[19]

Art. 6. The Insufficiency of the Existent Methods of Publicity

As this first period drew to a close, it became increasingly evident that, in spite of twelve centuries of effort to stamp out

---

[17] Wernz-Vidal, *Jus Canonicum,* V, n. 529.

[18] Council of London, 1102,—Baronius, *Annales,* XVIII, 132; *Constitutiones Ecclesiasticae* of Colloman, King of Hungary, 1103, l. ii, c. 9—Mansi, XX, 1179. With regard to this latter law, some authors maintain that it was aimed at curbing clandestine marriage, while others see in it a plan to prevent the marriage of Christians with the infidels then numerous in Hungary.

[19] Thus, Gratian, in *Causa XXX,* q. 5; Peter Lombard, *Liber IV Sent.,* D. 39; Bernardus Papiensis, *Summa de Matrimonio,* n. 14—Laspeyres ed., p. 304.

clandestinity, the abuse had survived. In fact, if the renewed interest manifested by legislators in the years just preceding the Fourth Lateran Council and at the Council itself can be taken as an indication of conditions, secret marriages were occurring more frequently. Without wishing to add unduly to the already staggering total of effects charged to the Crusades, it is probably true to say that the unsettled habits formed in men by those great movements made the situation so acute, that ecclesiastical authority was driven to find some more effective stay on clandestinity. If it had not been for the Crusades, canon law might have drifted on with its old inadequate regulations, even down to the Council of Trent itself.

And it is undeniable that, though various other causes may be alleged to explain the failure of the previous laws against secret marriage, the chief reason is to be found in the inadequacy of the laws themselves. For the most part, they were only local regulations, and were not always enforced even where they did exist. They were so vague that they could be easily evaded, and lacked sanctions sufficient to guarantee their observance.

The thirteenth century opened up a new era for canon law. The study of the science had been revived at the Universities, and scholars bent every energy to develop it. Their activities bore abundant fruit, and among other accomplishments, they soon provided the Church with a new and more suitable remedy for the malady of clandestine marriage.

CHAPTER II

THE FIRST PERIOD OF THE LEGISLATION ON THE BANNS

The first laws which expressly command the publication of proposed marriages date from the thirteenth century. The banns, then, are an innovation of the golden age of Canon Law.

Art. 1. The Derivation of the Word "Banns"

The word "banns" was not itself native to the Latin tongue, but was borrowed from the German,—at least according to the more common opinion among etymologists. Skeat[1] traces the history of the word from the old high German *bannen,* or *pannen,* meaning "to summon." It then passed into the medieval Latin and old French as *bannum,* or simply *ban.* This in turn found its way into Anglo-Saxon usage under the form *gebann,* and with the meaning of "exile," or "excommunication."

Whatever of its ancient lineage, it was in frequent use in France before the time of the Fourth Lateran Council, and it was from the French that Pope Innocent III took the term.[2] The word had several more or less related denotations: jurisdiction, and the territory over which the jurisdiction was to be exercised; the exercise of jurisdiction through a public edict; the edict issued by one having jurisdiction; and the penalty for the transgression of the law laid down in an edict.[3]

---

[1] *Etymological Dictionary,* v. "Banns." He notes that other scholars connect the word with the Latin "fama," and assign it an origin in the Sanskrit "bhan," meaning "to speak."

[2] C. 27, X, *de sponsalibus et matrimoniis,* IV, 1: " . . . bannis (ut tuis verbis utamur) . . . ". Soto also remarks this in *IV Sent.,* D. 28, q. 1, a. 1: "Bannum quippe non est latinum nomen, sed ex Gallico factitum."

[3] Wetzer und Welte, *Kirchenlexikon,* I, 1965—66, v. "Bannum"; Du Cange, *Glossarium,* I, 976, v. "Ban."

When the pre-nuptial announcement of marriage became customary in the diocese of Paris about the beginning of the thirteenth century, the term *banna* was also used to designate that type of proclamation. Then the Lateran Council universalized the practice, and the name was likewise generally adopted.

Certain of the older canonists see in the use of the word, not the sense of "proclamation," but rather its other signification of "penalty." This would then refer to the punishments attached by the Lateran decree to the violation of the law, or those added to it by local councils subsequently. Thus Hostiensis:[4] . . . *et vocabantur banna, quia et sub banno et sub poena excommunicationis dicebat sacerdos quod nullus hoc impedimentum celaret. . . .* This was probably the reason why the older canonists preferred the terms *denunciationes, publicationes,* and *proclamationes;* although they sometimes made use of the word *banna* in their matrimonial treatises, they employed it more frequently in the tracts dealing with crimes and penalties.

The English derivative of *banna* was at first "ban," or "bane"—used only in the singular, and pronounced with the long "a" sound. Since the sixteenth century, the word has been used in the plural form—due perhaps to the more definite legislation of the Council of Trent on the number of publications—and the long vowel pronunciation has given way to the present sound value.[5]

The banns may be described as the public announcements, made in the church, of a future marriage, for the purpose of bringing to light any obstacles which stand in the way of the union.[6]

Art. 2. Their Beginnings in Local Legislation

It is quite well agreed among authors that the credit for inaugurating the practice of publishing before the assembled congregation the names of those about to enter into marriage

---

[4] *Commentarium,* on c. 27, X, *de sponsalibus et matrimoniis,* IV, 1; also the Glossa on the same chapter.

[5] Murray, *New English Dictionary,* v. "Banns."

[6] Cappello, *De Sacramentis,* III, n. 159.

should go to Odo, Bishop of Paris.[7] There are some dissenters. Knecht and Schnitzer both pass over the Paris synod in silence, and concede the honor to the Council of London, held in 1200.[8] Sohm, and it seems Howard also, claim that the banns are an ancient institution in the Church, dating from the fifth century.[9] Even De Smet[10] hints that the banns enjoy a much greater antiquity than is generally attributed to them, basing his view on the prescriptions of certain old Rituals reproduced by Marténe. It is quite likely that, in preceding centuries, the parochial investigation often took the form of a public inquiry, which naturally involved the public announcement of the marriage, but legislation directed primarily at the announcement itself is first found in this period.

That the banns were in common usage in certain parts of France by the year 1212 is evident from the letter to the Bishop of Beauvais from Innocent III.[11] The practice was probably observed in parts of Italy also before the Lateran Council.[12]

Art. 3. The Fourth Lateran Council

The value of the new mode of publicity was soon perceived,

---

[7] *Synod. Constitut. Odonis, Episcopi Parisian.*, c. vii, n. 1—Mansi, XXII, 679. Cfr. Benedictus XIV, ep. "*Paucis abhinc,*" 19 Mart. 1758—*Coll. P. F.*, #380; Wernz, *Jus Decretalium*, IV, 179; Gasparri, *De Matrimonio*, n. 149; Fourneret, *Le Mariage Chrétien*, p. 94; Scherer, *Handbuch*, II, 146; Tournely, *Praelectiones*, p. 385, although he assigns the date as 1207.

[8] Knecht, *Handbuch des Kath. Eherechts*, p. 170; Schnitzer, *Handbuch des Kirchenrechts*, p. 122, n. 1. (This latter volume is not available, and the assertion is made on the statement of Fourneret, *op. cit.*, p. 94.) The Council of London referred to ordered the banns (in the eleventh chapter of its decrees) under the form of a triple publication.—Mansi, XXII, 946.

[9] Sohm, *Eheschliessung*, p. 175; Howard, *History of Matrimonial Institutions*, II, 360.

[10] De Smet, *Betrothment and Marriage*, (2 ed.), I, 24. His references to Marténe may be found in the *De Antiquis Ecclesiae Ritibus*, I, part 2, 627, 637, and 640.

[11] C. 27, X, *de spons. et mat.*, IV, 1. The text as given in the *Compilatio IV*, c. 2, *de clandest. mat.*, IV, 1 brings this fact out more clearly: ". . . bannis secundum consuetudinem ecclesiae Gallicanae editis . . ."—Augustinus, *Antiquae Collectiones*, p. 142.

[12] C. 8, *de test. et attest.*, II, 13, in *Compilatio I*—Augustinus, *op. cit.*, p. 29.

and at the General Council of the Fourth Lateran, 1215, it was extended by law to the universal Church.

Cum inhibitio copulae conjugalis sit in ultimis tribus gradibus revocata, eam in aliis volumus districte servari. Unde praedecessorum nostrorum vestigiis inhaerendo, clandestina conjugia penitus inhibemus: prohibentes etiam, ne quis sacerdos talibus interesse praesumat. Quare specialem quorumdam locorum consuetudinem ad alia generaliter prorogando: Statuimus, ut cum matrimonia fuerint contrahenda, in ecclesiis per presbyteros publice proponantur, competenti termino praefinito: ut infra illum qui voluerit et valuerit, legitimum impedimentum opponat: et ipsi presbyteri nihilominus investigent utrum aliquod impedimentum obsistat. Cum autem apparuerit probabilis conjectura contra copulam contrahendam, contractus interdicatur expresse, donec quid fieri debeat super eo, manifeste constiterit documentis.[13]

This, together with the sanctions attached to it in subsequent paragraphs, was the charter given to the new institution by the Church.

It was hoped that this measure would cure the evils against which it was directed—the abuses arising from clandestine marriage,—yet it did not achieve complete success. Some improvement was effected, and supplementary local legislation stimulated; but, the general law labored under certain defects. First of all, the regulation was not sufficiently determined, and its application was in practice uncertain and intermittent. The number of publications, for instance, was left to the discretion of each pastor. Commentators were divided on the interpretation of the decree; some of them held that the law demanded at least two announcements, while others maintained that one sufficed to fulfill the minimum of the canon. The pastor who followed the latter view would eliminate the valuable factor of delay in awaiting reports of impediments. Furthermore, the questions arising about persons with more than one proper pastor were left untouched, and no provision was made for the granting of dispensations.[14]

[13] C. 51 of the Fourth Lateran Council; c. 3, X, *de clandestina desponsatione*, IV, 3.

[14] Esmein, *Le Mariage*, (2 ed.), p. 203; Vacant—Mangenot, *Dictionnaire*, v. ''Bans.''

ART. 4. SUBSEQUENT PARTICULAR COUNCILS

Local councils took up the task of making known the law of the banns, and of supplying more definite details in the legislation, according to the needs of their respective places. Many of these synods deserve little more than mention, because they merely restated the general law or added some minor circumstantial determination.[15] Others, though, inserted important provisions that were lacking in the law of the Lateran Council. The nature of these supplements indicates that the weaknesses of the decree of the General Council had been noticed and diagnosed, for some of the particular Councils directed their efforts at remedying the uncertainties of the common law, while the others were content to insure, by means of more drastic sanctions, the requirements of the Lateran decree.

The first progress was made in regard to the number of publications. In the initial legislation on the banns—at the Synod of Paris and the Council of London—the triple publication had been adopted. The Ecumenical Council, faced with the problem of imposing the law on the whole of Christendom, settled only the broad outline of the canons, and left the incidentals for diocesan enactments, including, as has been noted, the question of the number of announcements. In all probability, the usual practice was to make two or three announcements, but several local Councils found it expedient to add this determination as a part of their statutes.[16]

---

[15] Council of Bayonne, 1300, n. 71—Mansi, XXV, 72; Synod of London, 1328, n. 8—Harduin, VII, 1541; Synod of Lambeth, 1330, n. 61—Harduin, VII, 1541; Council of Salamanca, 1335, c. 9—Harduin, VII, 1792; Council of Dublin, 1351, n. 5—Mansi, XXVI, 121. The Synodal Statutes of Nevers, 1468, n. 59—Mansi, XXX, 356, forbade publication on any day but Sunday, while the Council of Exeter—Mansi, XXIV, 793, limited the available days to Sundays and feasts. The Council of Liége, 1287, *de mat.* c. 2, made specific regulations about the manner of making the publications: they were to be announced after the Gospel of the Sunday Mass—Mansi, XXIV, 904; the Council of Tournay, 1481, *de mat.*, c. 3, was even more exact—the banns were to be published at High Mass on Sundays, at the time of the Offertory, and from the pulpit. (Hartzheim, V, 525.)

[16] Synod of Treves, 1227, c. 5—Mansi, XXIII, 28; Prov. Council of Scotland, 1225, c. 65—Mansi, XXII, 1241; Council of Treves, 1310, n. 96

After the law had been in operation for some time, experience showed that another important omission had been made. The simple text of the conciliar decree did not provide for the cases of those who changed residence and acquired a new domicile shortly before marriage. Their intention to marry would be made known to the comparative strangers in the new parish and would not be brought to the attention of their former neighbors. During this early period, all but one of the Councils, which took up the problem, were satisfied with demanding a testimonial letter from the former pastor.[17]

The Lateran Council had enacted penalties to be incurred by those who transgressed its precept. The pastor who assisted at such unlawful unions was made liable to a three years suspension from office, and the contracting parties were subject to punishment at the discretion of the Bishop. The children of these marriages might also suffer, in consequence of their parents' neglect, the loss of the advantages of putativity.[18]

It became evident, in the course of time, that the sanctions appended to the common law were not sufficient to deter people from violating its mandates. The individual Bishops and particular Councils undertook to fortify the canons with additional legislation. Generally, this took the form of excommunication; in some places, *ipso facto,* in others, *ferendae sententiae;* sometimes, extending only to the parties, and sometimes including the priest and all other persons, who knowingly and freely assisted.[19] Not all Ordinaries, however, invoked the supreme pun-

—Mansi, XXV, 273; Council of Cologne, 1280, c. 10—Mansi, XXIV, 356; Council of Exeter, 1287, c. vii—Mansi, XXIV, 793; Council of Liége, 1287, *de mat,* c. 2—Mansi, XXIV, 904; Synod of London, 1460, n. 8—Hefele, VII, 153; Synod of Osnabrück, 1553, c. xi—Hartzheim, VI, 231.

[17] Synod of Treves, 1227, *loc. cit.;* Council of Chichester, 1289, c. 24—Harduin, VII, 1156; Council of Cologne, 1536, vii, c. 45—Harduin, IX, 2011; these Councils demanded a letter from the former pastor, certifying the freedom of the parties. The Council of London, 1460, ordered the publication of the banns in the old parish—(Hefele, VIII, 153).

[18] C. 3, X, *de clandestina desponsatione,* IV, 3. This matter shall be more fully treated in a later chapter.

[19] Constitutions of Bordeaux 1263, c. 5—Mansi XXIII, 1110; Council of Mayence, 1267, c. 1—Mansi, XXIII, 1262; Council of Cologne, 1280, c. 10—Mansi, XXIV, 356; Council of Cahors, 1289, c. 18—Mansi, XXIV,

ishment of excommunication. Fines were imposed in some instances,[20] and, in the diocese of Angers, it was the rule, that the church or chapel would be under interdict, where a marriage was celebrated without being preceded by the banns.[21] The most startling means of enforcement was adopted in the diocese of Nicosa, threatening the priest assisting at the marriage with incarceration.[22]

The Lateran Council made no reference, in its decree, to dispensations. Laws were seldom relaxed, at that time, by any authority, and the law of the banns was a general law, whose administration was reserved to the Holy See. In such cases of reservation, however, "this claim of exclusive power by the Popes was interpreted by the Decretalists in such a way as to permit the bishops to dispense whenever the power was explicitly or implicitly granted to them, when legitimate custom arose, or when the urgent necessity or good of the Church demanded it."[23] The Pontiffs probably recognized certain urgent cases, and permitted, by their own rescripts, the omission of the banns. Certainly the Bishops, and even lesser dignitaries in the Church, acquired the faculty—at least by custom—and began to grant dispensations from this obligation. The Council of Treves, in

From about the beginning of the fifteenth century, there is

1012; Council of Padua, 1351—Mansi, XXVI, 234; Council of York, 1367, c. ix—Harduin, VII, 1792; Prov. Council of Angers—1448, n. 12—Mansi, XXXII, 89; Council of Avignon, 1509, n. 28—Mansi, XXXII, 546; Synod of Osnabrück, 1533, c. xi—Hefele, IX, 868.—The Council of Arles, 1260, c. iv—Harduin, VII, 512; Prov. Council of Lyons, 1449, n. 14—Mansi, XXXII, 97; and, the Synod of Cologne, 1527—Harduin, VI, 219—enacted the same penalty of excommunication, but made it *ferendae sententias.*

[20] Synod of Mausmünster, 1339, nn. 38-40—Hefele, VI, 647; Council of Avignon, as cited in the note above; this fine was an optional added penalty.

[21] Prov. Council of Angers, as above.

[22] Council of Nicosa, 1351—Mansi, XXVI, 315.

[23] O'Neill, *Papal Rescripts of Favor,* p. 38.

1310, referred to this power, but as something already possessed by the Bishop.[24]

[24] Council of Treves, 1310, n. 96—Mansi, XXV, 273.

evidence of abuses in the exercise of this faculty. Laments were uttered by several Councils over the scandals arising because of the indiscreet use of dispensations, and Ordinaries were cautioned to be slow in granting these favors, and to give them only when one or two publications had already been made.[25] Two synods went so far as to punish those who dispensed too freely, by placing them under interdict *ab ingressu ecclesiae,* for the space of one month.[26]

As a result of the growing frequency of partial dispensations —that is, dispensations from one or two of the three customary publications—a new point was introduced in the jurisprudence of the banns. To permit the marriage to take place immediately after one announcement would hardly conform to the letter of the general law,—(*competenti termino praefinito: ut intra illum . . . legitimum impedimentum opponat . . .*) and would certainly violate its spirit and purpose. Accordingly, legislators set about to remedy this situation, by insisting that there be some interval between the last announcement and the marriage itself.[27]

* * * * *

Such was the state of the canon law on the banns of marriage at the opening of the Council of Trent. The Lateran Council had put a new weapon at the Church's disposal in her warfare on clandestinity. Throughout the following centuries, experiments were carried on, the various Councils contributing to the

---

[25] Council of Paris, 1429, c. 32—(Harduin, VIII, 1050); Council of Lyons, 1449, c. 14—(Mansi, XXXII, 97); Synod of Soissons, 1457—(Hefele, VIII, 97); Synod of London, 1460, c. 8—(Mansi, XXV, 139); Council of Constance, 1463, *De Spons. et mat.*—(Hartzheim, V, 465); Council of Salzburg, 1490—(Mansi, XXXII, 412).

[26] Council of Paris, 1429, *loc. cit.;* Synod of Sens, 1461, art. iv, c. 4—Mansi, XXXII, 427. The Council of Paris indicated that Archdeacons and others were enjoying the power of dispensing.

[27] The Council of Exeter, 1287, demanded the space of eight days. (Mansi, XXIV, 795.) Three days were regarded as sufficient by the Council of Salzburg, 1490—Mansi, XXXII, 412; and by the Council of Narbonne, 1553, c. 53—Mansi, XXXIII, 1250. A somewhat similar rule was adopted by the Council of Mayence, 1549, c. 38—Harduin, IX, 2011—namely, that three successive calendar days were not to be used for the three publications.

perfection of the legislation. Nevertheless, it was becoming quite evident that the banns, by themselves, could not eliminate the evil of occult marriage. Marriages were contracted without the publications, in spite of all precepts and penalties.[28] In fact, in certain Spanish dioceses, notwithstanding an *ipso facto* excommunication in each case, the banns were never published, had not been for over a century, and the law served merely as a source of scandal. Sotus pleaded for its repeal.[29] The time had come for a sterner measure,—and the Council of Trent employed it, in its decree, "*Tametsi.*"

---

[28] Council of Freising, 1480—Hartzheim, V, 522: "Experientia magistra dicimus . . . quod decretum Concilii generalis de clandestina desponsatione, in nostris civitate et diocesi, per abusum in oblivionem venit, et observatum non existit." Also: the Council of Constance, 1463, c. *de spons. et mat*—(Hartzheim, V, 465); and the Council of Salzburg, as in the preceding note.

[29] The Bishops, he claimed, were using the law as a source of revenue. Before granting absolution from the censure incurred by omitting the banns, they demanded a donation to pious causes. Sotus, *Comment. in IV Sent.*, D. XXVIII, q. 2, a. 2.

CHAPTER III

THE LATER HISTORY OF THE BANNS

Art. 1. The Council of Trent

The statement has been made that the Council of Trent robbed the banns of much of their importance, when it demanded, as a condition for validity, that the marriage be celebrated before the pastor and witnesses.[1] This assertion is not entirely true. While it is a fact that both of these requirements were aimed at the elimination of clandestine marriage, nevertheless they accomplish their purpose in different ways. The Council of Trent really gave new life to the legislation on the banns, and enhanced the value of the publications by the more accurate definition it gave to the obligation, when in the chapter *"Tametsi"* it declared that:

> . . . Wherefore, treading in the steps of the Sacred Council of Lateran celebrated under Innocent III, it ordains that, for the future, before a marriage is contracted, the proper parish priest of the contracting parties shall three times announce publicly in the Church, during the solemnization of mass, on three continuous festival days, between whom marriage is to be celebrated; after which publication of banns, if there be no lawful impediment opposed, the marriage shall be proceeded with in the face of the church; . . .[2]

This new law on the banns was subject also to the clause appended to the decree "Tametsi," and therefore, went into effect only in those parishes, in which it was published. It happened, in some places, that the section of the Tridentine decree on the banns was published, but not the part dealing with the form of marriage. Wherever the law of the Council of Trent did not become effective, the regulations of the Fourth Lateran

---

[1] Vacant—Mangenot, *Dict. Theol. Cath.*, art. "Bans."

[2] Council of Trent, Sess. XXIV, *de ref. mat.*, c. 1; Waterworth, *Canons and Decrees of the Council of Trent*, p. 197.

Council remained in force, together with whatever local laws and customs existed in that region.[3]

The period between the Council of Trent and the Code did not witness any change in the general law—and the Code itself practically reproduced the Tridentine legislation on the banns. The intervening epoch was one of explanation rather than innovation. Synods and canonists concerned themselves with correctly interpreting a regulation already satisfactorily developed. In this lay a marked difference from the preceding era, when the endeavor had been to formulate and enforce a suitable law. The Council of Trent solved both of these problems. It gave the Church a very determined norm for the publication of marriage, and, by insisting on a juridical form of marriage, it indirectly provided for the observance of the banns, because it forced the parties to bring their matrimonial plans to the attention of their proper pastor.

The decree of the Council of Trent was much clearer than that of the Lateran Council, and the circumstances of publication were more exactly delineated. But this very improvement made necessary a more accurate interpretation, and controversies soon arose among the authors. Such a difficulty was to be expected, and the Church had anticipated it. By the constitution *"Alias nos,"*[4] Pius IV instituted a commission of eight Cardinals to interpret the disciplinary decrees of the Council of Trent. Much of the post-Tridentine history of the banns centers around this Congregation. Gradually its decrees settled disputed points and built up the background for the present law. To undertake a chronological account of these declarations would be a task monotonous and misleading. They are intimately connected with the canonical disputes which they dealt with, and therefore shall be discussed in conjunction with those controversies.

---

[3] Benedictus XIV, ep., *"Paucis abhinc,"* 19 Mart. 1758—Fontes, #447. The decree *"Tametsi"* could also become effective through usage.

[4] Pius IV, const. *"Alias nos,"* 2 Aug. 1564—*Bullar. Rom.* VII, 300. The commission was known as the Sacra Congregatio Cardinalium Sancti Concilii Tridentini Interpretum, or more commonly, Sacra Congregatio Concilii.

Art. 2. The Controversies on the Interpretation of the Law

a. *The Application of the Term Proprius Parochus*

In its decree "*Tametsi,*" the Council of Trent decided that the publications were to be made by the proper pastor of the parties. "Although it was not decreed who the proper pastor was, immediately after the Council canonists unanimously determined that he was the pastor of the place in which the contracting parties had a domicile. . . . Domicile was defined, in general, as the place of permanent habitation. . . . Canonists generally acknowledged three distinct kinds of domicile, *viz.,* the domicile of origin, the domicile of habitation, and the legal or necessary domicile." The domicile (or place) of origin was defined as the place in which one was born, that is, according to the more common view, the place of legal birth, where the paternal domicile was located at the time of birth. The domicile of habitation was determined by residence in a certain locality, coupled with the intention of remaining there forever; and legal or necessary domicile was defined as, "that which one necessarily obtains by disposition of law, either by reason of bond with another person (*mulier nupta*), by reason of an office *per se* permanent (*clericus beneficiatus*), or by reason of one's condition or state of life (*relegatus, filiusfamilias*)."[5] Besides domicile, quasi-domicile also sufficed to give one the status of a parishioner—at first, this was only a probable opinion, but later it became certain. The exact nature of quasi-domicile was disputed by the commentators, until the congregation of the Holy Office described it, in a letter of 1867, as being constituted by residence in a place, together with the intention of remaining there for the greater part of a year.[6]

Under the law of the Council of Trent, therefore, the banns had to be proclaimed by that pastor in whose parish the parties had a domicile or quasi-domicile. The case of those who had not acquired either of these, shall be considered later, but here it might be well to mention the peculiar and short-lived excep-

---

[5] Costello, *Domicile and Quasi-Domicile,* pp. 44-46, 49, 52, 57.

[6] S. C. S. Off., litt. encycl., 7 Jun. 1867—*Coll. P. F.,* #1407; Costello, *op. cit.,* 73-88.

tion Vermeersch[7] deduced from the decree *"Ne Temere."* He claimed that, according to the new general law, and apart from local legislation and custom, the determining factors were not domicile and quasi-domicile, but domicile and month's residence, and the reason he alleged was that quasi-domicile had been suppressed in all matters pertaining to matrimony. De Smet,[8] however, pointed out that the elision of quasi-domicile extended only *ad licitam matrimonii celebrationem,* and did not affect its power to determine parochial affiliation.

"That an individual might have more than one domicile at the same time was one of the earliest notions concerning domicile taken for granted in canon law."[9] Either or both of the parties to a marriage might have acquired more than one domicile or quasi-domicile, and that situation would be particularly confusing in regard to the banns. As far as the celebration of the marriage was concerned, it was quite evident that the marriage could be contracted before only one of the several proper pastors; but in deciding the extent of the obligation to publish the banns, the solution was not so easily available. It was conceded, by most of the authors, that the prenuptial investigation should not be confined to one domicile, nor even to all domiciles retained at the time of marriage, but should be carried on in the parishes of former residence. However, in supplying definite rules to cover the various cases of plurality of domicile, authorities differed widely.

First of all, it happened very frequently that the two parties did not live in the same parish. The majority of canonists agreed that the law demanded the proclamation of the banns in the parishes of both parties.[10] In some places, though, the

---

[7] *De Forma Sponsalium et Matrimonii post Decretum "Ne Temere," Appendix de bannis,* #65.

[8] De Smet, *Betrothment and Marriage,* I, 46. He cites *N. R. T.,* XLI [1909], 178, and *Rev. Clerge Fr.,* LVII [1909], 353.

[9] Costello, *Domicile and Quasi-Domicile,* p. 55.

[10] Sanchez, *De Mat.,* III, d. 6, n. 41; Barbosa, *De Officio Episc.,* alleg. xxxii, n. 7; Schmalzgrueber, *Jus Eccl.,* IV, iii, n. 13; Gonzalez Tellez, *Comment. Perpet.,* IV, iii, n. 7; Bangen, *Instructio Practica,* I, 312; Tourneley, *Praelect. Theol.,* p. 390; Reiffenstuel, *Jus Can. Univ.,* IV, iii, nn. 8; Feije, *De Imped. et Dispens.,* I, n. 251; Scavini, *Theol. Moralis,* IV,

practice was in vogue, so Pirhing maintained, of publishing the banns in only one of the parishes, the parish, namely, where the marriage was to take place. Pirhing[11] hesitated to condemn this interpretation, arguing that custom could derogate from human laws. Later commentators, Wernz especially, abandoned this tolerant attitude, and strongly denied the legality of the practice.[12] While advocating in general the common teaching that the banns should be published in both parishes, Lehmkuhl sponsored the peculiar exception, that, if the parishes were adjoining (*valde vicinae*) it was necessary to make the publication in only one of them.[13]

Canonists encountered still greater difficulty, and ventured the most divergent answers in interpreting the obligation of the law in cases where one or both of the parties had changed his or her domicile shortly before the publication of the banns was requested. This problem differed in principle from that of plurality of domicile, though in reality it was closely related to it. The question here was whether the banns should be published in the actual domicile of habitation, or in the previous, but no longer maintained domicile, or in both. Observing the strict letter of the law, the publication was to be made in the proper parish, namely, wherever the person had a domicile (or quasi-domicile) at the time of publication, and only in that place. Therefore, according to the literal interpretation of the decree of the Council of Trent, the banns would have to be published in the newly acquired parish, even if the party was in residence there only one day, and absolutely unknown; whereas, there would be no obligation to make any announcement in the parish he had recently left, though it had been his home for years.

Pontius[14] thought it enough to observe the letter of the law.

616; Smith, *Rights and Duties of Parish Priests,* IV, n. 658; Deshayes, *Questions Pratiques sur le Mariage,* n. 123; Gasparri, *De Mat.,* n. 162; Wernz, *Jus Decret., IV,* 186; De Smet, *Betrothment and Marriage,* I, 46; Zitelli, *Apparatus Juris Eccl.,* p. 402.

[11] *Jus Canon.,* IV, iii, n. 4, #28.

[12] Wernz, *Jus Decret.,* IV, 186.

[13] Lehmkuhl, *Theol. Moralis,* II, 478.

[14] *Tractatus de Sacramento Matrimonii,* V, c. 30, n. 5.

Deshayes[15] agreed with that view in theory, that it would be quite sufficient to publish the banns in the newly acquired domicile, provided that the *examen de statu libero*[16] was observed; in practice, nevertheless, he counseled the announcing of the banns in both old and new parishes, because the formal examination was not everywhere enforced.

Most commonly, the authors held that the banns were to be published in the new parish,[17] and also in the parish which the party had but recently left. In determining how soon the obligation to publish the banns in the former parish ceased, much was left to local custom and episcopal regulation.[18]

The Roman practice demanded the banns in the old parish during the first two months after the change of residence, and in the new parish only when that length of time had been completed.[19]

The German and Austrian usage was, that after six weeks in the new home, it was sufficient to publish the banns in that place; before the completion of the six weeks, it was necessary to make the announcements in both the new and the old parish.[20]

In several dioceses, the rule held that the banns were to be published in the parish of actual residence, and in the former parish also, until six months had elapsed after the change of domicile.[21] Another plan was devised in the province of Naples,

---

[15] *Questions Pratiques*, n. 126.

[16] The process outlined in the Instruction of the Holy Office, "*Cum alias,*" 21 Aug. 1670—*Bullar. Rom.*, XVIII, 81.

[17] Engel, *Collegium Univ. Juris Can.*, p. 320; Schmalzgrueber, *Jus Eccl.*, IV, iii, n. 15; Carriere, *Praelect. Theol.*, III, 387, Vechiotti, *Institut. Can.*, p. 103; Wernz, *Jus Decret.*, IV, 199; Gasparri, *De Mat.*, n. 163; De Smet, *Betrothment and Marriage*, I, 46. A few commentators disagreed: Sanchez, *De Mat.*, III, d. 6, n. 6; Barbosa, *De Off. Episc.*, alleg. xxxii, n. 14; Bangen, *Instructio Practica*, I, 32 regarded publication in the old parish sufficient, until one month had elapsed after the change of residence. The Council of Albi, 1850, ruled that the obligation of making the announcements in the new parish did not begin before the completion of the sixth month there.—*Coll Lac*, IV, 1118.

[18] Lehmkuhl, *Theologia Moralis*, II, n. 674, 4.

[19] Wernz, *Jus Decret.*, IV, 187.

[20] *Instructio Austriaca*, n. 62—*Coll. Lac.*, V, 1294; *A. k. KR.*, LII [1909], 300.

[21] Prov. Council of Rheims, 1849, XI, iii—Coll. Lac., IV, 126; Prov.

whereby one publication was made in the new parish, and two in the old, until four months after the change of residence.[22]

The commentators were influenced by the practice of their own dioceses, with the result that they gave forth a variety of opinions; generally, though, the maximum period during which they regarded the obligation as effective in both parishes ranged between six months and a year. And even when the new domicile had been that long established, canonists advised the use of further precaution, by obtaining testimonial letters from the pastors of all parishes in which either party had lived for a considerable length of time, during the several years preceding the proposed marriage.[23] They regarded this as especially urgent when the residence had been in a different diocese; and in that case, they could appeal for support to an instruction of the Congregation of the Holy Office, demanding a formal inquiry into the free state of the parties, to be conducted before the Ordinary, and to be certified by him.[24]

St. Alphonsus held that the banns should also be published in the parishes where the parties were born, even though they no longer retained their domiciles—voluntary or necessary—in those places.[25] The basis of the view was that such a procedure would bring the proposed marriage to the attention of relatives and friends who were well acquainted with the parties.

The general law, as proposed by the Council of Trent, was silent on this question, and, although in certain cases the arguments advanced by St. Alphonsus would urge the adoption of his view, they were not of universal application. It often hap-

---

Council of Sens, 1850, III, viii—*Coll. Lac.*, IV, 894; Prov. Council of Bourges, 1850, de mat.—*Coll. Lac.*, IV, 1118; *Decreta Cong. Archipresbyterorum*, Mechlin, 1851—Dens, *De Spons. et Mat.*, p. 50; Prov. Council of Quebec, 1854, xiii, n. 4—*Coll. Lac.*, III, 648.

[22] Prov. Council of Naples, 1699, III, iv, n. 5—*Coll. Lac.*, I, 198.

[23] Bangen, *Instructio Practica*, I, 37; Wernz, *Jus Decretalium*, IV, 187; Deshayes, *Questions Pratiques*, 126.

[24] S. C. S. Off., instr., "*Cum alias,*" 21 Aug. 1670—*Bullar. Rom.*, XVIII, 81. There was a similar instruction issued in 1890 by the Holy Office, August 22, 1890.—*Coll. P. F.*, #1740—dealing more directly with the question of the banns.

[25] St. Alphonsus, *Theologia Moralis*, VI, n. 991, #2.

pened that the parties had left their birthplace in infancy, in which event the banns would be superfluous. Most of the other authors disagreed with St. Alphonsus, and maintained that, under the common law, it was unnecessary *per se* to publish the banns in the place of origin.[26] They admitted, nevertheless, that, under certain conditions, publication of the banns in the place of origin would be at least advisable, for example, in the case of *vagi,* or when the parties had only recently left the parish of birth. Then too, they all recognized the right of the local Ordinary to order publication in the domicile of origin, if it also was within his diocese. In three of the four published cases submitted to the Sacred Congregation of the Council, the answer was that the proclamation of the banns was unnecessary in the place of origin; and in the fourth, it seems from the context of the decree, that the parish in question was, not only a domicile of origin, but also of actual habitation.[27] The common opinion also received the support of the Holy Office, in an instruction given in 1890:

> Publicationes faciendae sunt in loco domicilii, vel quasi domicilii. Expedit etiam [hence not a strict obligation], ut fiant in loco originis, si contrahentes ibidem morati fuerunt post adeptam aetatem ad matrimonium contrahendum idoneam; atque insuper in locis ubi saltem per decem menses commorati fuerunt, nisi jam a pluribus annis domicilium fixerint in loco, ubi matrimonium contrahendum est.[28]

Besides the foregoing general determinations of the law of the banns, special rules were formulated for certain classes of people.

---

[26] Reiffenstuel, *Jus Can. Univ.*, IV, iii, n. 14; Schmalzgrueber, *Jus Eccl.*, IV, iii, n. 21; Feije, *De Imped. et Dispens.*, I, n. 251, #4; Bangen, *Instructio Practica*, I, 39; Zitelli, *Apparatus Juris Eccl.*, p. 402; De Becker, *Praelectiones Canonicae*, p. 250; Deshayes, *Questions Pratiques*, n. 137; Gasparri, *De Mat.*, n. 163; Wernz, *Jus Decret.*, IV, 188.

[27] The decisions declaring such publication unnecessary were: S. C. C., *Terra Guastaldi,* 1579 (no date given),—Zamboni, *Collectio Declar. S. C. C.*, II, 408, n. 2; S. C. C., *Vercellen.*, 6 Maji 1719—*Thes. Res. S. C. C.*, I, 183; and S. C. C., *Senogallien,* 3 Apr. 1734—*Thes. Res. S. C. C.*, VI, 244. The other decree referred to was: S. C. C., *Senogallien.*, 29 Jan. 1684—Zamboni, *loc. cit.*, n. 5. Cfr. Ballerini-Palmieri, *Opus Theologicum Morale*, VI, 429.

[28] S. C. S. Off., 22 Aug. 1890—*Coll. P. F.*, #1740.

It was forbidden to publish the banns for the marriage of a non-diocesan, until the permission of the Bishop had been obtained. This license was not to be granted until a diligent investigation had been instituted.[29]

The Tridentine law made similar provision for the marriages of *vagi*—that is, those with no settled home. The Ordinary's permission had to be obtained, and when given, the banns were to be published in the place where the *vagus* was actually staying, since that was his proper parish.[30] Because the *vagus* would generally be unknown in that place, authors deemed it almost imperative that the banns be also announced in his domicile of origin, and in any place where he had remained for a rather long period of time after reaching marriageable age.[31]

Minors were placed in a separate category. During their minority, they retained a legal or necessary domicile in the parish of their parents, and the banns were published in that place. Some of the authors computed minority according to the civil law, while others adhered to the old Roman method; at times, however, the local legislation determined this point.[32]

Some canonists treated the cases of soldiers, and of domestic servants as special problems.[33] In reality, though, as Deshayes noted,[34] they did not merit this particular classification; therefore, unless local law imposed additional obligations, the banns

---

[29] S. C. Ep. et Reg., 20 Dec. 1692—Ferraris, *Prompta Bibliotheca*, art. "Matrimonium," iv, n. 30; and the Holy Office decrees of 1670 and 1890 already cited.

[30] Council of Trent, Sess. XXIV, *de ref. mat.*, c. 7.

[31] St. Alphonsus, *Theologia Moralis*, VI, n. 1089; Lehmkuhl, *Theologia Moralis*, II, n. 674; Deshayes, *Questions Pratiques*, p. 137; Wernz, *Jus Decretalium*, IV, 188.

[32] Thus, the Prov. Council of Sens, 1850, defined minors as being males under 25, and females under 21; if they were without relatives in the ascending line, they attained majority at 21 years of age. (*Coll. Lac.*, IV, 894.) This definition corresponded to that of the French civil law. Much the same rule was laid down by the Prov. Council of Quebec, 1854, xiii, *de sac. mat.*, n. 5—*Coll. Lac.*, III, 648.

[33] Lehmkuhl, *Theologia Moralis*, II, n. 674: soldiers were to be regarded as having a domicile of law in the place where they lived previous to enlistment.

[34] *Questions Pratiques*, p. 138.

would have to be published in their place of garrison or employment, if they had a domicile or quasi-domicile there; in their legal domicile, if they were minors; and in their domicile of origin, if the case warranted it, according to the norms already described.

b. *The Circumstances of Publication*

The law definitely stated that the banns were to be published in the church (*in ecclesiis*). It was only natural that the church should be chosen, because the faithful of the parish gathered there every Sunday. Several authors regarded it as also permissible to announce the banns outside the church building itself, on the occasion of a procession or some other public religious function, at which the members of the parish were present in large numbers.[35] Gasparri[36] suggested that it would be better to consult the Ordinary, if time permitted, before adopting this course, which was contrary to the letter of the law; and Deshayes[37] further advised the pastor to inform the people of the reason he had for following such an unusual procedure, lest they be scandalized at his action.

By the term "church" was understood the parochial church. If there were other oratories in the parish—as for example, hospital chapels, or churches (non-parochial) confided to the care of religious—the banns were not to be published in them, unless they were serving temporarily as the parish church.[38]

When there was, within the confines of the parish, a chapel of ease—that is, an annexed or vicarial chapel, which, with the approbation of the Bishop, was assigned officially as the center of religious services for a determined territory,—a difficulty arose with regard to the publication of the banns. In certain

---

[35] St. Alphonsus, *Theologia Moralis*, VI, n. 991; Sanchez, *De Mat.*, III, d. 6, n. 9; Pirhing, *Jus Can.*, IV, iii, n. 14, #28; Scavini, *Theologia Moralis*, IV, 615; Kenrick, *Theologia Moralis*, II, 310.

[36] *De Mat.*, n. 169.

[37] *Questions Pratiques*, p. 107.

[38] Bangen, *Instructio Practica*, II, 45; Gasparri, *De Mat.*, n. 169; Wernz, *Jus Decretalium*, IV, 196; Deshayes, *Questions Pratiques*, p. 108.

places in Germany and Austria,[39] due to custom and local legislation, when a resident of such an annexed territory wished to be married, it was necessary to announce the banns both in the chapel and in the parochial church. This custom and legislation was regarded by canonists generally, as being *praeter legem,* and they maintained that, wherever that particular regulation did not exist, it sufficed to proclaim the banns for those people in the chapel alone, provided that the chapel had its own distinct territory.[40]

The Congregation of the Council adopted the same view in one of its decisions,[41] namely, that since the annexed church had its own distinct district, it would be sufficient to publish the banns for the people of that place in the chapel only. The Congregation made it clear, however, that its answer was influenced by the facts of the particular case, and was, therefore, applicable to it alone.

* * * * *

According to the meagre regulations of the Lateran decree, the number of publications had been left to the judgment of the priest. He was to make the public announcement,[42] and then set a period of time during which the people could advance information about any canonical impediments which stood in the way of the marriage. Where the Tridentine law had not become effective, and was not supplied by local legislation, the Lateran decree was the only legal provision in force even down to the Code itself. Thus, in many places one publication sufficed.[43] Under the law of the Council of Trent, on the other hand, the banns had to be published three times. Perhaps this

---

[39] Bangen, *Instructio Practica,* II, 45.

[40] Carriere, *Praelect. Theol.,* III, 386; Deshayes, *Questions Pratiques,* p. 107; De Smet, *Betrothment and Marriage,* I, 48; Wernz, *Jus Decretalium,* IV, 184.

[41] S. C. C., *in causa Colonien.,* 23 Feb. 1901—*Thes. Res. S. C. C.,* CLX, 129.

[42] Hostiensis, *Summa Aurea,* p. 335, held that two publications were necessary, because the word *banna* was used in the plural.

[43] Gasparri, *De Mat.,* n. 161; Wernz, *Jus Decretalium,* IV, 183; Vechiotti, *Instit. Canon.,* III, 102; De Smet, *Betrothment and Marriage,* I, 49.

was another demonstration of the old axiom: *Omne trinum perfectum,* but there was also a practical motive behind it. The delay involved would give the friends and neighbors of the parties time in which to learn of the wedding, and raise any just objection they might have; besides, it would afford the parties an opportunity to consider the importance of the step they were taking, and avoid a hasty ill-mated marriage.

The days chosen by the law were the feast days of precept, general or particular, because of the gathering of the people in the church on those days. The more solemn feasts, Christmas, Easter, and Pentecost, were excluded by custom in many dioceses, and in certain places, particularly in Germany, Advent and Lent were *tempora clausa* not only for the solemnization of marriage, but also for the banns.[44] In fact, in some dioceses, it was customary to limit publications to Sundays.[45]

After the suppression of certain feasts of precept, the question arose about the availability of those days for the proclamation of the banns. The suppression had removed the obligation of assisting at Mass, but the feasts were still observed with the old liturgical solemnity, and the faithful persisted in the pious practice of hearing Mass. It was this circumstance that prompted the inquiry from the theologians about publishing the banns.

Two early decisions by the Congregation of the Council, meant only as particular answers, gave a strict interpretation of the Tridentine law. The Bishop could, in virtue of the powers given him by the Council of Trent, permit by dispensation the use of those feasts, but he should do so only in individual cases, and for grave reasons.[46]

Authors generally handled the problem more leniently. Carriere,[47] it is true, was for strict observance of the letter of the law, and excluded the days of precept suppressed by the Concordat of 1802 (with France), but he based his view on the

---

[44] Bangen, *Instructio Practica,* II, 44; Feije, *De Imped. et Dispens.,* I, n. 241; Ferraris, *Prompta Bibliotheca,* art. "Matrimonium," iv, n. 22.

[45] Lehmkuhl, *Theologia Moralis,* II, n. 673.

[46] S. C. C., *Brunen.,* 17 Jan. 1780—Zamboni, *Collectio Declar. S. C. C.,* II, 408; and S. C. C., *Tudert.,* 19 Apr. 1823—*Thes. Res. S. C. C.,* LXXXIII, 76.

[47] *Praelect. Theol.,* III, 383.

French tradition of rigor, engendered by the civil law on the banns. The others favored the use of suppressed feast days still solemnly celebrated, and on which the people continued to attend Mass. The Bishop, they held, could permit this practice even habitually.[48] A later decision of the Congregation of the Council adopted the common opinion.[49]

The same principle was applied by a number of canonists, with regard to publishing the banns on ferial days. They argued that if the spirit of the law of the Council of Trent could prevail over its letter in one case, it could likewise do it in a similar case.[50]

The Congregation had insisted on two things in the other question, the solemnity and the attendance. On those days on which there was no solemnity, there would not be the likelihood of having a large number of the parishioners present, but, granting that this gathering of the people was had, due, for example, to the presence of a prominent preacher, could the banns be published? Many of the ablest canonists maintained the affirmative, that the banns could be published.[51] They argued that the restriction placed by the Council of Trent was merely to insure general knowledge, and that, when this was equally or better secured in some other way, the regulation did not have to be observed.

The other side was just as zealous for the letter of the law. They contended that the Council must have foreseen all the

---

[48] Feije, *De Imped. et Dispens.*, I, n. 244; Gasparri, *De Mat.*, n. 166; De Becker, *Praelect. Can.*, p. 249; Scavini, *Theologia Moralis*, IV, 901; Wernz, *Jus Decretalium*, IV, 194; Lehmkuhl, *Theologia Moralis*, II, n. 673; Ojetti, *Synopsis Rerum Moralium*, III, 331.

[49] S. C. C., *Pinarolien.*, 7 Apr. 1862—*Zamboni*, *Collectio Declar. S. C. C.*, II, 409.

[50] Under ferials, they also included, for the purposes of this discussion, the feast days which had never been of precept—the profestal days.

[51] Sanchez, *De Mat.*, III, d. 6, n. 9; Barbosa, *De Off. Episc.*, alleg. xxxii, n. 15; (these two limited the use to profestal days, and excluded ferials in the strict sense); Engel, *Collegium Univ. Juris Can.*, p. 320; Reiffenstuel, *Jus Can. Univ.*, IV, iii, n. 7; Schmalzgrueber, *Jus Eccl.*, IV, iii, n. 24; Deshayes, *Questions Pratiques*, p. 111; Grandclaude, *Jus Can.*, III, 54; Konings, *Theologia Moralis*, n. 1535; Kenrick, *Theologia Moralis*, n. 311.

advantages of ferial publication, and yet refused to endorse it.[52] Nevertheless, most of these theologians admitted that the Bishop could permit the use of a ferial day in a particular case; some few, however, denied even this concession.[53]

The Tridentine law insisted that, once the publications had been begun, no feast day be allowed to pass without an announcement being made.[54] The purpose of that specification was to prevent the pastor from delaying the marriage too long, and also to forestall any danger of the people forgetting their duty of reporting impediments in time. When three feast days of precept followed each other in immediate calendar succession, some authors denied that the pastor could take advantage of them to make all three required publications.[55] Such a procedure, they held, would practically nullify the purpose of the law, and therefore was forbidden by it. Wernz,[56] on the other hand, maintained that such a prohibition, however desirable, could not be deduced from the general statute, which clearly stated that the days should be in uninterrupted succession, and the restriction would be effective only if local custom or legislation had introduced it. The ideal, therefore, was to have the days of publication close enough to one another to avoid undue delay of the marriage, and yet not so close as to render the banns almost useless.

* * * * *

[52] Gonzalez Tellez, *Comment. Perpetua*, IV, iii, n. 7; Vechiotti, *Institut. Can.*, III, 107; Feije, *De Impcd. et Dispens.*, I, n. 246; Wernz, *Jus Decretalium*, IV, 183. They also appealed to the special permission granted to the Vicars Apostolic of India, enabling them to permit publication of ferials when necessary. The rescript referred to was an instruction of the Congregation of the Propaganda, dated Sept. 8, 1869. (*Collectio Constitut., Decret., etc. ad Usum Societatis Missionum*, #846.)

[53] Ferraris, *Prompta Bibliotheca*, art. "Matrimonium," iv, n. 17 and 18: Bangen, *Instructio Practica*, II, 45, held that the Congregation of the Council would prefer the granting of a dispensation from the publication to the permission to transfer the obligation to a ferial day.

[54] Certain exceptions introduced in various places have already been noted.

[55] Gasparri, *De Mat.*, n. 165; St. Alphonsus, *Theologia Moralis*, n. 992.

[56] *Jus Decretalium*, IV, 183.

The Council of Trent had also commanded that the publications be made during the celebration of Mass. The Mass preferred was the parochial one, that which was more solemnly celebrated, and at which most of the parishioners were present.[57]

Though the Tridentine decree indicated that the Mass was the proper occasion for the publication of the banns, most of the earlier theologians countenanced publishing them at Vespers, and at other sacred functions, provided always that there was present a large gathering of the parishioners. However, they insisted that there be some just cause to justify this departure from the letter of the law.[58] The Congregation of the Council permitted the change, if there was reason for making it.[59] The later canonists seem to have been a little stricter on the matter; they held that the announcements were not to be made outside of Mass, unless there was necessity for so doing, or unless a dispensation had been obtained.[60] The Bishop could grant the favor even habitually, as for instance, if the Vespers were better attended, but the pastor himself could not take that liberty with the law.

c. *The Form of the Publications*

Neither the Lateran nor the Tridentine law had chosen any formula for the publication of the banns. The wording of the announcement could take any form, as long as it identified the contracting parties. The Roman Ritual described a method for making the proclamation, but did not impose it as obligatory;

---

[57] In conventual churches, it was the pastor's choice to publish the banns either at the conventual, or at the parochial Mass, provided that the *concursus populi* was had at the one chosen.—S. C. C., *Novarien.*, 8 Jul. 1724 —*Thes. Res. S. C. C.*, III, 48.

[58] Sanchez, *De Mat.*, III, d. 6, n. 9; Barbosa, *De Off. Episc.*, alleg. xxxii, n. 5; Gutierrez, *Liber Tertius Canon. Quaest.*, 172, n. 7; St. Alphonsus, *Theologia Moralis*, VI, n. 991.

[59] S. C. C., *Avenion.*, 25 Oct. 1586—Zamboni, *Collectio Decret. S. C. C.*, II, 408; Zamboni quoted the answer as: *Posse ex gratia;* Bangen, *Instructio Practica*, II, 46 claimed that the authentic reading was: *Posse ex causa.*

[60] De Smet, *Betrothment and Marriage*, I, 50; Wernz, *Jus Decretalium*, IV, 184; Deshayes, *Questions Pratiques*, p. 110; Synod of Fort Wayne, 1903, c. vii, n. 165—*Synod. Dioc.*, p. 61.

the exact determination was left to custom and local law. Generally the announcements contained mention of the names and parishes of the parties, their state of life—single or widowed—how far the publications had advanced, and included a reference to the duty of revealing impediments, incumbent on those who knew of their existence.

The Council of Trent had evidently meant that the publications be proposed orally, and that was the way in which commentators interpreted the decree. It seems, however, that even before the time of the Council, the banns were published in certain places by posting the names of the contracting parties on the church doors.[61] The Council of Naples in 1699 ordered the observance of the practice in that province, in addition to, not in place of, the vocal publications.[62] It was not until 1908 that the Church permitted the substitution of the written for the oral notice.[63]

d. *The Causes Excusing from the Publications*

Grave urgency furnished one reason for proceeding to the celebration of marriage without the banns. This necessity was verified, whenever the wedding could not be deferred long enough to make the publications, nor even long enough to reach the Superior competent to dispense. Theologians obliged the pastor to notify the Bishop about the matter as soon as possible, and he would either order the proclamation of the banns before the consummation of the marriage, or grant a dispensation.[64]

---

[61] Barbosa, *Collectanea Doctorum*, on c. 2, X, IV, *qui filii legitimi*, n. 17.

[62] Prov. Council of Naples, 1699, III, c. ix, n. 3—*Coll. Lac.*, I, 198; likewise, I Prov. Council of New Granada, 1868, t. IV, c. 11—*Coll. Lac.*, VI, 521.

[63] S. C. C., *Parisien.*, 28 Mart. 1908—*A. S.*, XLI [1908], 246. The notice was to be posted on three consecutive Sundays, from the time of the early Mass to the last evening service. The rescript limited the use of this method of publication to the larger parishes. The original grant was to last for ten years, but by the end of that period the Code had been promulgated, and it gave the Bishops even wider faculties in the matter.

[64] St. Alphonsus, *Thelogia Moralis*, VI, n. 991; Gasparri, *De Mat.*, n. 154; De Smet, *Betrothment and Marriage*, I, 53; Feije, *De Imped. et Dispens.*, I, n. 267.

Custom had secured for royalty the privilege of exemption from this law. For the common people, the banns were about the only efficient way of making the proposed marriage public, whereas princely weddings were state affairs, widely heralded. Impediments to royal marriages could hardly remain occult. Even at the time that Hostiensis was writing his treatises,[65] this prerogative was accorded them. The later writers retained the tradition, and it has continued in existence even down to the present.[66]

At mixed marriages, the omission of the banns was not merely permitted, but was positively commanded. On this point, more will be said in a subsequent chapter.

The chief title to exemption from the obligation of the banns was dispensation. Under the Lateran law, as it was established by the Council, only the Pope could dispense, because it was a general law, and no provision had been made in it for the dispensation from its articles at the hands of inferiors of the Roman Pontiff. However, long before the Council of Trent, the Bishops were dispensing, and it was recognized that they had acquired this faculty through custom.[67] After the Council of Trent, Ordinaries enjoyed the power of dispensing in virtue of an express provision contained in the decree itself. The Prelates included in the term "Ordinary" were, according to the commentators, for their respective territories: Residential Bishops, Abbots and Prelates Nullius, Vicars Capitular, the Chapters, in the interim before the selection of the Vicar Capitular, and Vicars General. Some canonists questioned the power of the Vicar General, unless he had obtained a special mandate from the Bishop,[68] but the more common and probable opinion held that he could dispense without such special delegation, the argument being that the title "Ordinary" extended to Vicars Gen-

---

[65] Hostiensis, *Summa Aurea*, p. 335.

[66] Wernz, *Jus Decretalium*, IV, 181; Gasparri, *De Mat.*, n. 154; Scavini, *Theologia Moralis*, III, 897; Deshayes, *Questions Pratiques*, p. 104.

[67] Mazzaeus, *De Matrimonio Conscientiae*, c. ii, n. 4; Sanchez, *De Mat.*, III, d. 7, n. 1; Schmalzgrueber, *Jus Eccl.*, IV, iii, n. 25.

[68] Pontius, *Tractatus de Sacramento Matrimonii*, V, 31, n. 5; Menochius, *De Arbitrariis Judicum*, c. 69, n. 5.

eral, as custom clearly showed.[69] All admitted that the Bishop could curtail this power at will. Barbosa,[70] while admitting that the Vicar General could himself dispense from the banns, denied him the right to give a general delegation of this authority.

There were theologians who even doubted, or limited, the power of the Bishop himself to delegate others to dispense from the banns. Menochius[71] held that Ordinaries had been chosen *industria personae,* and that therefore they could not commit the faculty of dispensing to others. A few authors taught that the Bishop could give a general delegation only to his Vicar General, but the common opinion defended the Bishop's ability to permit any of the clerics of the diocese to dispense, even habitually.[72]

Vicars Forane did not enjoy the faculty of dispensing, nor did pastors, unless it had been specially committed to them by the Ordinary.[73] Authorities admitted though, that they could declare that the law did not bind in a particular case, in which the celebration of marriage was so urgent as to allow no time to request a dispensation from the Bishop.

Canonists were divided when it came to defining the jurisdiction possessed by Ordinaries with regard to dispensing from the publications to be made in the domicile of the party who was not their subject. The more common view was, that the dispensation from the Bishop of one party would be operative in the dioceses of both parties.[74] The intrinsic argument advanced

---

[69] Sanchez, *De Mat.*, III, d. 7, n. 10; Pirhing, *Jus Can.*, IV, iii, n. 12; St. Alphonsus, *Theologia Moralis,* VI, n. 1007; Tourneley, *Praelectiones Theol.*, III, 395; Santi, *Praelectiones Juris Can.*, IV, iii, n. 11; Gasparri, *De Mat.*, n. 182; Dens, *De Sponsalibus et Matrimonio,* p. 51; and others.

[70] *De Off. Episc., alleg.* xxxii, n. 37.

[71] *De Arbitrariis Judicum,* c. 69, n. 55.

[72] Sanchez, *De Mat.*, III, d. 7, n. 20; Schmalzgrueber, *Jus Eccl.*, IV, iii, n. 20; Gutierrez, *Liber Tertius Can. Quest., tract. de mat.*, c. lvi, n. 13; *Instructio Austriaca,* n. 83—*Coll. Lac.*, V, 1296.

[73] Sanchez, *loc cit.*, n. 17; Gutierrez, *loc cit.*, n. 11; Fagnanus, *Comment. in IV Librum Decret.*, c. iii, *de cland. despons.*, nn. 4-8; Gonzalez—Tellez, *Comment. Perpetua,* IV, iii, n. 7; Reiffenstuel, *Jus Can. Univ.*, IV, iii, n. 39.

[74] Canchez, *De Mat.*, III, d. 7, n. 9; Gonzalez—Tellez, *Comment. Perpetua,* IV, iii, n. 7; Reiffenstuel, *Jus Can. Univ.*, IV, iii, n. 36; Schmalzgrueber,

was that the unity of the contract and the connection of the parties to it made a non-diocesan subject to that Bishop, who granted the dispensation. The advocates of this view appealed to a decision of the Congregation of the Council[75] as upholding them, but the defenders of the opposite opinion claimed the support of the very same response.

The other side of the question had its champions too,[76] who denied the validity of arguing from the unity of contract and connection of persons; each party, they held, was entirely independent of the other in the matter of the publications, and subject each to his or her own Ordinary in obtaining dispensations from the banns. They further claimed that the reasons which moved one Bishop to relax the law for his subject would not necessarily exist for the other party, thus rendering the dispensation unjustified when applied to that other person.

This dissension among the doctors at least gave occasion for a doubt of law, and the first opinion was recognized as being safe in practice.[77] This held especially for those dioceses in which custom sanctioned the practice, and also where the Bishops of the respective dioceses had agreed to empower each other to dispense.[78]

One author[79] called attention to a somewhat related problem.

Jus Eccl., IV, iii, n. 25; D'Annibale, *Summula Theologiae Moralis,* III, n. 452; Lehmkuhl, *Theologia Moralis,* II, n. 864; Gasparri, *De Mat.*, n. 183; Vecchiotti, *Institutiones Canonicae,* III, 105; Wernz, *Jus Decretalium,* IV, 190.

[75] S. C. C., 20 Apr., 1606—Giraldi, *Expositio Juris Pontificii,* II, 114. The decree declared that dispensations should be sought from the Ordinaries of both parties, or at least, that a testimonial letter of free state, from the second Bishop, be presented to the one dispensing.

[76] Pontius, *Tractatus de Sacramento Matrimonii,* V, c. 31, n. 9; Scavini, *Theologia Moralis,* IV, 623; Feije, *De Imped. et Dispens.*, I, 262; Carriere, *Praelectiones Theologicae,* III, n. 428; von Scherer, *Handbuch des Kirchenrechts,* II, 151; *N. R. T.*, I [1856], 452; and the *I. E. R.*, XVI, series 3, [1895], 1135, which advised this course, though admitting the probability of the opposite view.

[77] Gasparri, *De Mat.*, n. 183 invoked the principle: *Ecclesia supplet.*

[78] Thus, the Bishops of the Province of Albi—Prov. Council of Albi, 1850, t. V, decr. IX, n. 3—*Coll. Lac.*, IV, 435. Von Scherer, *Handbuch des Kirchenrechts,* II, 157 noted the same practice in Germany.

[79] Carriere, *Praelect. Theol.*, III, n. 433.

It was admitted that one became subject to a Bishop by establishing a domicile or quasi-domicile in his diocese. But, according to many theologians, there was no obligation to publish the banns in a parish where residence had only just been established; the publications were, in such a case, to be made in the former parish. This determination had even been made part of the law in certain places, as has already been noted. Supposing that the previous residence had been in a different diocese, to which Ordinary would application for dispensation be made—the Bishop to whom the party was there and then subject, by reason of domicile, or to the Bishop of the old domicile, in whose territory the banns were to be published, but who could no longer claim jurisdiction over the party? The author who raised the question favored the competency of the latter, on the ground that the law of the banns was to be treated as a territorial law.

* * * * *

In treating of the dispensation itself, canonists differed very little. The dispensation could be given in various ways; it might be given totally—from all publications, or the obligation might be only reduced, to one or two proclamations. The Council of Trent allowed the Ordinary to adopt another course, and merely postpone the announcements until after the celebration of the marriage. Furthermore, it was quite certain that the Bishop could dispense with some of the formalities, such as the restriction to days of precept, during Mass, *et cetera.* At times, the law was relaxed by statute, reducing the number of publications necessary in seldom visited outmissions; this was done in several American dioceses.[80] Generally, though, dispensations were given in particular cases.

Before the dispensation could be given, sufficient reason had to be advanced to justify the relaxation of the law. The Superior was bound to verify the truth of the alleged cause, and was

[80] III Synod of New York, 1868, c. VI, de Mat., n. iii—*Collectio Synodorum Archidioecesis Neo Ebor.*, p. 38; Synod of Baltimore, 1853, n. xiii—*Synodus Diocesana*, p. 29; II Synod of Leavenworth, 1887, c. XXII n. 2, #119—*Decreta Synod, Dioces.*, p. 51; Synod of Fort Wayne, 1903, c. VII, n. 169—*Synodus Dioces*, p. 61.

further obliged to have moral certainty as to the absence of impediments. At least, if he had a positive doubt about the freedom of the parties, he coud not, with a clear conscience, dispense from all three publications.[81]

Theologians quite agreed that an Ordinary who dispensed from all publications, without a serious cause, would be guilty of grave sin.[82] Sometimes, rescripts were given, as it was said, *sine causa;* this term merely meant that the favor was granted for a cause other than those usually advanced.[83]

Authors enumerated various causes, which, in their opinions, would justify the granting of a dispensation. The Council of Trent referred to dispensing when there was fear of unjust interference with the marriage. This was not to be understood as the only admissible reason.[84] Among the other causes frequently mentioned by canonists were: Danger of infamy to the parties, if the marriage were delayed for the banns; the approach of Advent or Lent, during which seasons the solemn celebration of marriage was forbidden; danger of civil marriage; the noble rank,[85] or special merit of one or both of the parties; and, the necessity of celebrating marriage without further delay, as for instance, in the case of soldiers going to war.

Some authorities hesitated to accept any cause not included in the commonly recognized categories,[86] but others agreed that any reason the Bishop judged as sufficient, could be resorted to, since the Council of Trent had committed the whole matter to

---

[81] Sanchez, *De Mat.*, III, d. 8, n. 4; Schmalzgrueber, *Jus Eccl.*, IV, iii. n. 25.

[82] Benedictus XIV, ep. encycl. "*Nimiam licentiam,*" 18 Maii 1743—Fontes, #337.

[83] Carriere, *Praelectiones Theol.*, II, 1112.

[84] St. Alphonsus, *Theologia Moralis*, VI, n. 1005; Grandclaude, *Jus Canonicum*, III, 56; Vechiotti, *Institutiones Canon.*, III, 104; Gasparri, *De Mat.*, n. 187.

[85] That is, those of noble rank, who were not princes; noblemen of princely rank were regarded as exempt.

[86] Those advanced by approved authors, and especially ones, applicable to the banns, contained in the Instr. of the Cong. of the Propaganda, May 8, 1877—*Coll. P. F.*, #1470; and that of the Apostolic Datary—*A. S.* XXXIV [1901-1902], 34-35. Thus, the Bishop of Passau insisted on the presentation of canonical causes only. (*Ak K. R.*, LIII [1909], 739.)

his prudence.[87] It was even held, that a dispensation could be given at the mere request of the parties, if the Bishop had moral certainty of their freedom to marry.[88]

There was a gradation of causes, a more serious cause being required for the omission of two publications than for one, and a very serious reason was needed to justify a total dispensation.[89]

Canonists sought to draw a line of distinction between cases where the Bishop would be bound to dispense, and those in which he might do so. Barbosa held that the Bishop was obliged to grant a dispensation from the banns, whenever a just cause existed;[90] most theologians, however, admitted that there were instances when the Bishop would be free to grant the favor, or to withhold it. When the dispensation from the banns would entail a notable good, or avert a notable loss, then the Bishop was obliged to grant the favor; otherwise, not. If the Bishop denied the dispensation when he was not bound to give it, nothing could be done about it, because he merely refused a benefit of law to which the parties had no right; but if the cause was one of those recognized as obliging the Bishop to use his faculties, authors maintained that there was room for appeal to the next higher superior, *in devolutivo tantum*.[91] Sanchez even went so far as to permit the priest to assist at the marriage without the banns, on the ground that the Ordinary was to be considered as granting that which he unjustly refused.[92]

The faculty of dispensing would be gravely abused by a Bishop, who would grant a dispensation from the banns to minors, when he knew that their parents were justly opposed to the marriage. For, one of the chief aims of the legislator in

[87] Schmalzgrueber, *Jus Eccl.*, IV, iii, n. 37; Gutierrez, *Liber Tertius Can. Quest.*, tract. de mat., c. lvii, n. 3; Grandclaude, *Jus Canonicum*, III, 57; Deshayes, *Questions Pratiques*, p. 162; Gasparri, *De Mat.*, n. 185.

[88] Gasparri, *loc. cit.; A. E. R.*, XXIII [1900], 418.

[89] Benedictus XIV, ep. encycl., "*Nimiam licentiam,*" 18 Maii 1743, nn. 13-15—*Fontes*, #337; D'Annibale, *Summula*, III, n. 453, #7.

[90] *De Off. Episc.*, alleg. xxxii, n. 51.

[91] Barbosa, *De Off. Episc.*, alleg. xxxii, n. 51; Bangen, *Instructio Practica*, II, 52.

[92] *De Mat.*, III, d. 10, n. 8.

instituting the banns had been precisely to avoid the scandals and discord such marriages produced.[93]

Dispensations were to be given *gratis*. The Council of Trent had insisted on that reform, and had devoted one of its chapters to forbidding the imposing of fees for dispensations.[94] This was followed by the famous decree, known as the *Taxa Innocentiana*,[95] which contained the same prohibition, and reprobated all contrary customs. Local synods frequently called attention to these declarations, notably the Third Plenary Council of Baltimore.[96]

e. *The Sanctions Attached to the Law*

The Council of Trent did not abrogate the punishments established by the decree of the Lateran Council for those who violated the law of the banns. These penalties remained part of the written law even down to the Code itself,[97] and continued to engage the attention of the canonists. During the latter part of the last century, however, these sanctions were seldom enforced, and came to be regarded as obsolete.[98]

The decree of the Lateran Council had stipulated that the pastor, who assisted at a bannless marriage, or culpably permitted the marriage to take place, should be suspended *ab officio* for the period of three years; and the Bishop was empowered to increase the penalty if the case warranted this.[99] The same punishment was imposed on any other priest who assisted at such marriages.[100]

---

[93] Cosci, *De Sponsalibus Vota Decisiva*, IX, n. 8, p. 191.

[94] Council of Trent, Sess. XXIV, *de ref. mat.*, c. 5.

[95] Innocentius XI, instr., 8 Oct. 1678—*Bullar. Rom.*, XIX, 105.

[96] III Prov. Council of Milan, 1572, c. xvii—Mansi, XXXIV, 577; S. C. de Prop. Fide, 12 Feb. 1821—*Coll. P. F.*, #755; III Plen. Council of Baltimore, c. IV, n. 134; *A. E. R.*, III [1890], 16.

[97] Canon 6, n. 5. The sanctions attached to the law on the banns were not affected by the constitution "Apostolicae Sedis," because they were not *latae sententiae.*

[98] Deshayes, *Questions Pratiques*, p. 99.

[99] C. 3, X, *de clandestina desponsatione*, IV, 3.

[100] Giraldi, *Expositio Juris Pont.*, II, 508, noted that if the priest had no office, the Bishop could inflict some other suitable penalty. Covarruvias and others held that the penalty also entailed suspension *a beneficio*, but

Canonists asked if the duration of the punishment could be reduced at the discretion of the superior imposing it. Hostiensis[101] maintained that the judge or Ordinary had no choice but to impose the sentence as laid down in the law. The question was more fully discussed by authors under a slightly different aspect, that is, whether a Bishop, who had already inflicted the suspension on one of his priests, could dispense that priest from the punishment before the three years had been accomplished. Hostiensis,[102] in this case, would allow the Bishop to relax the penalty, arguing that when the general law did not reserve the power to dispense from punishments, by that very fact it empowered Ordinaries to release from them. The opposite view was defended, among the earlier theologians, by Sanchez and Covarruvias.[103] Their stand was that the Bishop could not dispense from a suspension, when the time limit had been set by common law; not because of any reservation by the superior, but on account of the time determination in the law itself. Most of the later authors adopted the same view.[104]

The pastor was not the only one liable to punishment. The contracting parties could be subjected to grave penalties, at the discretion of the Bishop. Furthermore, if the marriage happened to be nullified by some impediment,[105] the parties would encounter much greater difficulty in obtaining a dispensation from that impediment,[106] and consequently in having their marriage revalidated. This was likewise a penal measure, based on the principle that those who despise the Church's salutary precepts were to be deemed unworthy of her favors.

The witnesses to the marriage were not burdened with any

Sanchez, *De Mat.*, d. 52, n. 4; Barbosa, *Collectanea Doctorum,* IV, iii, n. 19, and Wernz, *Jus Decretalium,* IV, 182, denied such an extension.

[101] *Summa Aurea,* p. 336.

[102] *Summa Aurea,* p. 336; also, Grandclaude, *Jus Canonicum,* III, 71.

[103] Sanchez, *De Mat.*, III, d. 52, n. 2; Covarruvias, *Opera Omnia, de mat.*, p. II, c. vi, n. 16.

[104] Benedict XIV, *De Synodo Diocesana,* XII, c. 6, n. 2; Schmalzgrueber, *Jus Eccl.*, IV, iii, n. 87; Feije, *De Imped. et Dispens.*, I, n. 263; Gasparri, *De Mat.*, n. 171; Wernz, *Jus Decret.*, IV, 182; Kober, *Suspension,* p. 129.

[105] St. Alphonsus, *Theologia Moralis,* VI, n. 990 limited it to marriages invalidated by an impediment of consanguinity or affinity.

[106] Council of Trent, Sess. XXIV, *de ref. mat.*, c. 5.

penalty according to the common law, but canonists recommended that they should not be allowed to escape unpunished, for by their cooperation they had rendered the unlawful marriage possible.[107] Soto[108] took exception to this conclusion, holding that since the general law had not decreed a punishment for them, the Bishops should likewise refrain from doing it. The Sacred Congregation of the Council, in one of its responses,[109] recognized the right of the Bishop to take action against all those assisting at the marriage, parties, priest and witnesses.

The children born of these clandestine marriages were liable to be handicapped by illegitimacy. They encountered this disfavor of law, not as a penalty, but in consequence of their parents' neglect, for, bannless marriages, if invalid, were not regarded as putative.

In the course of its development, canon law evolved the principle of putativity,[110] whereby the offspring of an invalid marriage contracted in good faith and celebrated *in facie ecclesiae*, enjoyed the privilege of legitimacy, just as did children born of a valid marriage. An invalid marriage remained putative as long as one of the parties to it was in ignorance of the impediment which rendered the marriage null. This provision of putativity found its basis in natural equity, for it was recognized as being out of all proportion to place children begotten of a merely material fornication on the same level as those conceived in formally sinful intercourse.

But, embodied in the Decretals, there was a special and explicit exception to this principle: those who contracted marriage, without observing the formalities of the banns, forfeited

---

[107] Sanchez, *De Mat.*, III, d. 46, n. 5; Benedict XIV, *De Synodo Diocesana,* XII, c. 6, n. 2; Gasparri, *De Mat.*, n. 172; De Smet, *Betrothment and Marriage,* I, 46.

[108] *Comment. in IV Sent.,* d. 28, q. 2, a. 2. It is quite possible that he was influenced in his view by the abuses then current in Spain, for he refers to the charges made against the authorities of avidity in collecting fines.

[109] S. C. C., 10 Feb. 1629—Ferraris, *Prompta Bibliotheca, art. ''Matrim.,''* ix, n. 1, p. 365.

[110] The first clear cut, definite reference to it is made by Rolandus, *Summa,* p. 231.

for their children the privilege of putativity.[111] Therefore, whenever the bannless marriage was also invalid, because of some impediment,[112] the children born of it were illegitimate. Ignorance of the impediment on the part of one, or even of both parents did not save the children from this handicap. In fact, even if the parents had pursued the most diligent private investigation as to their free state, and were convinced that there were no impediments to their marriage, even in that case, according to the opinion of most of the canonists, the same fate befell the offspring.

There was a two-fold reason for this regulation of law. First, an invalid marriage, according to the definition of canonists, could be putative only, if it had been celebrated *in facie ecclesiae,* and most of them doubted that a marriage entered into without the banns measured up to this requirement.[113] The

[111] C. 3, X, *de clandestina desponsatione,* IV, 3. Panormitanus, in his *Commentaria,* on this chapter (n. 9), held that the words of the Decretals: "*hujusmodi clandestina . . . conjugia,*" referred only to secret marriages, and therefore, did not apply to those celebrated publicly, before a multitude of the faithful, even though the banns were omitted.

[112] According to the prevalent opinion, this defect of legitimacy occurred when the marriage was invalid, no matter from what impediment the obstacle to validity arose—provided that it was such that the banns could have brought it to light. If the impediment could not have been discovered, even if the banns were published, authors agreed that the offspring escaped this provision of law, for the parents were not guilty of affected ignorance, and the purpose of the provision had ceased. Thus, Sanchez, *De Mat.,* III, d. 42, n. 4; Barbosa, *Collectanea Doctorum,* on c. 3, X, *de cland. desp., IV,* 3; Mascardus, *Conclusiones Probationum Omnium,* Con. 798, n. 6; Schmalzgrueber, *Jus Eccl.,* IV, iii, n. 77. Hostiensis, *Summa,* p. 336 and Pontius, *Tract. de Sac. Mat.,* V, c. 27, n. 7 limited the range of this prescription even further, arguing from the words "in gradu prohibito" that it applied only to those marriages invalidated by an impediment of cansanguinity or affinity. Covarruvias, *Opera Omnia,* tract. de mat., c. vi, n. 11, excluded from the effects of this decree those marriages, which were contracted in danger of death for the purpose of legitimating children of a previously concubinary union.

[113] A few of the older authors regarded a bannless marriage as being "in facie ecclesiae," if it took place before a number of the faithful—thus, Panormitanus, *Commentaria,* on c. 3, X, *de clandestina desponsatione,* IV, 3, n. 9; Mascardus, *Conclus. Probat.,* con. 798; n. 7; Durandus, *Speculum Juris,* IV, iv, *de cland. desp.* After the Council of Trent had established

second and weightier motive for depriving bannless marriages of the favor of putativity was this, that those who neglected a precaution so important as the banns gave evidence of affecting ignorance. One who did not employ the means of inquiry easily at his command was regarded as preferring ignorance.[114] The legislator adopted the position[115] that ignorance of an existing impediment could be excused, if one pursued the investigation the law deemed necessary, whereas it would lose all shred of inculpability, when one proceeded in disregard or contempt of the law. When, therefore, two persons married without attending to the law of the banns, the legislator judged them guilty of affected ignorance, and, in case there was some impediment present which invalidated the marriage, the law presumed that they had positive knowledge of that impediment. Suarez[116] advanced the view that the omission of the banns gave a simple presumption of this knowledge, and that the status of the children really depended on the actual state of mind of the parents,—whether they actually were in good faith or bad. He stood alone for this opinion, which was manifestly opposed to the words of the law,[117] and the presumption was generally accepted as being *juris et de jure.*

Sanchez[118] took occasion to note that children born of an invalid marriage celebrated without the banns were in a worse predicament than those begotten in undisguised fornication. The latter might be easily legitimated through the subsequent marriage of their parents, whereas the former class was deprived of the legal favor of legitimation, by the Tridentine decree already referred to, which prevented the validation of their parents' attempted marriage.

---

its form of marriage, Suarez held that a marriage celebrated according to that norm was "in facie ecclesiae," despite the omission of the banns.—*Opera Omnia,* tom. 23, p. 2, *De Censuris,* disp. 50, *de irregularitate ex defectu natalium,* sect. 1, n. 10.

[114] St. Thomas, *Summa Theologica,* 1a, 2ae, q. 6, a. 8.

[115] C. 3, X, *de clandestina desponsatione,* IV, 3.

[116] Suarez, *loc. cit.*

[117] C. 3, X, *de clandestina desponsatione,* IV, 3: "de parentum ignorantia nullum habitura subsidium."

[118] *De Mat.,* III, d. 42, n. 2.

Under the conditions prevailing in the later centuries, the necessity of these sanctions diminished. With the introduction of the Tridentine form, insuring the intervention of the pastor at the celebration of the marriage, the law of the banns was, in all probability, better observed; then too, faculties to dispense from the banns were more widely distributed, and dispensations more freely given, making it unlikely that parties would choose to be married in outright neglect of the banns. At any rate, the general changes in the social and political order made the enforcing of these penalties less practicable. They lived on in books, rather than in events, until the Code of Canon Law wrote their epitaph in canon 6, n. 5.

Art. 3. The Legislation in the United States

According to the common law, wherever the prescriptions of the Council of Trent were not in force, the old legislation of the Lateran Council remained in effect. This rule, it seems, was not generally observed in the American missions,[119] until after the First Plenary Council. No doubt there was good reason for this apparent neglect. In the colonial days, some of the larger centers of population had resident pastors, but the more remote districts were visited by missionaries only at long intervals. To demand the banns in such cases would delay the marriages too long, and entail serious inconvenience for the parties. Then too, the isolation of those outposts of civilization rendered the banns less necessary; the concealing of an impediment incurred in the new community would be unlikely, and the discovery of one previously contracted impossible.

As soon as conditions permitted, the hierarchy took steps to bring about conformity with the general law. First of all, the Bishops assembled at the Sixth Provincial Council of Baltimore resolved to foster the inauguration of the practice;[120] then, at

---

[119] The decree "*Tametsi*" had been published in only a few dioceses. For a list of these places, consult the Third Plenary Council of Baltimore—*Acta et Decreta*, p. cvii.

[120] VI Prov. Council of Baltimore, 1846, iii—*Concil. Balt.*, p. 244: "Censuerunt Patres optandum esse ut, statim atque Ordinario uniuscujusque Dioecesis utile visum fuerit, proclamationes quae Banna vocari solent,

the First Plenary Council, the order was definitely promulgated that the banns were to be published in all the Provinces under the jurisdiction of the Council.[121]

However, even in the older and more settled eastern provinces of New York and Baltimore special exceptions had to be made to meet the existing conditions. Thus, at the diocesan synod of Baltimore in 1853, the year in which the law went into effect, the Archbishop ruled that the banns would have to be published only in parish churches where Mass was celebrated every Sunday. Marriages of slaves were exempted from the law, and extensive faculties were granted to the pastors for dispensing.[122] At the third Synod of New York,[123] pastors of parishes in towns and cities were admonished to make the three publications, but were given power to dispense from one of these proclamations. In country places, and wherever Mass was celebrated only infrequently, those exceptions from the law would be in effect which each pastor obtained by special grant.

---

habeantur et fiant ante celebrationem Matrimoniorum, juxta mentem Conciliorum Lateranensis et Tridentini.''

[121] I Plenary Council of Baltimore, 1852, n. ix—*Concil. Balt. Plen.*, p. 46: ''Statuunt Patres in omnibus harum Provinciarum dioecesibus, post festa paschalia anni proxime venturi, Banna matrimoniorum publicanda esse. Ordinarios vero hortatur ut ne hac in re, nisi gravissimis de causis, dispensent.''

[122] Synod of Baltimore, 1853, n. xiii.

[123] III Synod of New York, 1868, c. vi, n. 3—*Synodorum Archidioc. Neo Ebor. Collectio,* p. 38.

CHAPTER IV

THE PUBLICATION OF THE BANNS BEFORE MIXED MARRIAGES

The special legislation in regard to the banns in cases of mixed marriage is of rather late origin; in fact, the first general law on the subject is that of the Code itself.[1] At the time of the inception of the law of the banns, Europe was practically one in faith. There existed, it is true, heretical groups in different places, but they were small, short-lived, and isolated. The problem of providing for the announcement of marriages between Catholics and non-Catholics arose only much later in canonical history. Even after the Reformation, for nearly three centuries, there was no legislation on this point.[2] During that period, mixed marriages were very rarely permitted, and only in royal houses; and for princely marriages the banns were not usually published.[3] Towards the end of the eighteenth century the rigidity of this discipline was relaxed, and mixed marriages became more frequent. The priest's presence at such ceremonies, however, was merely tolerated, and his rôle reduced to the minimum.[4]

At first it was feared that the publication of the banns would seem to entail ecclesiastical encouragement of mixed marriages,

---

[1] Wernz-Vidal, *Jus Canonicum,* V, 139.

[2] There seems to have been no restriction at the time of Corradus, for, in recording a certain case of mixed marriage, he quotes the phrase: "in proclamationibus, juxta formam Concilii Tridentini fieri solitis. . . ."—(*Praxis Disp. Apost.,* l. vii, c. 2, n. 99).

[3] Benedictus XIV, ep. encycl., "Magnae Nobis," 29 Jun. 1748—*Bullar. Bened. XIV,* II, 547; *Canoniste Contemporain,* XVI [1893], 423.

[4] The term "passive assistance" is used in the decrees, sometimes in the strict sense of mere presence, sometimes in a wider sense, the restriction merely consisting in the prohibition of liturgical rites or the banns. Cfr. Schenk, *Matrimonial Impediments of Mixed Religion and Disparity of Cult,* p. 64, note 59.

and the result was that the banns were forbidden. This absolute, inflexible rule did not long survive. Within one year of its first appearance, it was altered, in answer to the entreaties of the Bishops of Belgium, where the civil law demanded the banns.[5] The conditions added to this first permission illustrate how grudgingly the Church gave Her consent; the publication could indeed take place, but only outside the church itself, in fact, outside the limits of the sacred precincts. Perhaps on account of the peculiar local circumstances attaching to the Mechlin decree, or maybe because experience proved this restriction too harsh, it was not added in the later decrees and instructions on this matter.

For more than a century thereafter, almost up to the period of the Code, the question of the announcing of marriages between Catholics and those of other religious beliefs frequently attracted the attention of the Roman authorities and of local legislators. In appreciating the Church's stand on this point, it must be remembered that she faced a dilemma. If the banns were published, the public good might suffer through a seeming approbation of indifferentism. If, on the other hand, the marriage was allowed to take place unannounced, there might be grave danger of its nullity. Circumstances, therefore, directed the decisions. If, in a given locality, non-Catholics were few in number—and thus conspicuous, and, if the State laws on divorce were strict, the Church would favor the omitting of the banns; because, the danger of scandal in such a case would be great, and the probability of impediment—at least, of *ligamen*, —rather slight. But, under the opposite conditions, the ecclesiastical authorities would be inclined to publish the banns. Civil law also played a part in determining the Church's position. For instance, in Germany, and in the realms under the

[5] Pius VI, rescript., "*Exequendo nunc*" (to the Archbishop of Mechlin), 13 Jul: 1782—*Fontes* # 471: "Quod attinet ad proclamationes . . . respondemus: cum praeordinatae sint ad futuram celebrationem matrimonii et ex consequenti positivam eidem cooperationem contineant, non posse nos ut hae fiant annuere."—In his letter of May 13, 1793, the Pontiff permitted: "ut eae fiant, non solum extra ecclesiam, sed etiam omnimodo extra locum sacrum." (Words taken from letter as cited in *Canoniste Contemporain*, XVI [1893], 423.

control of Joseph II and his successors, the secular power insisted so much on the banns, that the Church was forced to tolerate publication in order to avoid more serious evils.

The first rescript to outline a procedure resembling the present discipline was given in 1793, to the Duchy of Clèves, on the occasion of the extension of the Benedictine Declaration to that place.[6] The banns could be published, but no mention was to be made of the religion of the parties.

It became the practice to permit the banns at mixed marriages in those provinces where passive assistance was tolerated.[7]

In those regions which were predominantly Catholic, there was little need of a solution to this problem of the banns; as might be expected, therefore, the chief contributions to the development of the legislation came through Germany, Austria, and the United States, where the two groups, Catholic and Protestant, had strong representation. During the first three decades of the nineteenth century, the Holy See issued many decrees on the subject of mixed marriages,[8] but none of them, it appears, referred to the banns.

In a letter of 1830, Pius VIII seems to have regarded the publication of the banns as the usual course.[9] Such a deduction, though, may not be entirely justified, as the Pontiff's principal concern in writing the letter was the safeguarding of the prenuptial promises, or *cautiones* (the secular law had ordered that children be brought up in the religion of the father); the banns were referred to only incidentally. But the Church legislation on the banns was not left long in uncertainty. It was first decided that the banns should not be published if the required *cautiones* were not given;[10] then this norm was deserted, and the

---

[6] The Benedictine Declaration was the Constitution of Benedict XIV, "*Matrimonia,*" Nov. 4, 1741—*Coll. P. F.*, #333. The rescript to Cleves is found in *Thes. Res. S. C. C.*, LXII, 153.

[7] *N. R. T.*, XV, [1883], 590. Also, consult note 4, above.

[8] Roskovany, *De Matrim. Mixtis, passim.*

and Münster.

[10] Gregorius XVI, ep. encycl., "*Summo igitur,*" 27 Maii 1832, nn. 2 and 7—*Fontes*, # 484: ". . . Enimvero animarum curator, qui se aliter gereret,

[9] Pius VIII, litt. ap., "*Litteris altero,*" 25 Mart. 1830—*Coll. P. F.*, # 811; the letter was sent to the Ordinaries of Cologne, Treves, Paderborn,

proclamation of the banns was tolerated whenever the mixed marriage could not be prevented.[11]

The Church in Austria throughout this period was suffering under the tyrannical scourge of Josephism. When the civil legislator assumed the right of exercising ecclesiastical jurisdiction, the banns did not escape his prying eye and meddling edict. The imperial law insisted not only on the publication of the banns by the pastors of both parties, but on the still more detestable obligation of furnishing the *testimonium de peractis bannis* to a non-Catholic minister.[12] Under these circumstances, the Holy See adopted the policy of permitting publication, placing as the only restriction the usual prohibition of the mention of the difference of religion.[13] Later, decrees of the local councils—approved by Rome—commanded or supposed the announcement of the banns at mixed marriages.[14]

The decisions established for German and Austrian dioceses can hardly be regarded as indications of the true sentiments of the Church; they were evidently forced from her, under pressure of the civil law. In the United States, she encountered no such interference, and, notwithstanding a series of misunderstandings in the beginning, the American decrees became the measure and standard of the future legislation on the subject.

At the Sixth Provincial Council of Baltimore—at the time the province embraced the whole United States—it was decided that the practice of publishing the banns should be introduced by the Bishops.[15]

---

in praesentibus Bavariae adjunctis, approbare quodamodo illicitas illas nuptias facto suo videretur.''

[11] Gregorius XVI, instr. (ad Ordinarios Bavariae), 12 Sept. 1834—Zitelli, *Apparatus Juris Eccles.*, p. 403, n. 1; D'Annibale, *Summula Theol. Moralis,* III, n. 465.

[12] Von Scherer, *Handbuch des Kirchenrechts,* II, 160.

[13] Cfr. the letter of Cardinal Lambruschini, appended to the Apostolic letter of Gregory XVI, ''Quas vestro,'' addressed to the Ordinaries of Hungary, and dated April 30, 1841—*Coll. P. F.*, # 920, note on p. 519.

[14] Prov. Council of Gran, 1858, t. iii, c. *de mat mixtis—Coll. Lac.*, V, 27; Prov. Council of Prague, 1860, t. iv, c. 12, *de mat mixtis—Coll. Lac.*, V, 521; Prov. Council of Kalosca, 1863,—*Coll. Lac.*, V, 659.

[15] VI Prov. Council of Baltimore, decreta iii—*Concil. Prov. Baltim.*, p. 244.

Censuerunt Patres optandum esse ut, statim atque Ordinario uniuscujusque Dioecesis utile visum fuerit, proclamationes quae Banna vocari solent, habeantur et fiant ante celebrationem Matrimoniorum, juxta mentem Conciliorum Lateranensis et Tridentini.

The acts of the Council were submitted to the Holy See, and, after some delay, were approved. This fact was made known in two letters to Archbishop Eccleston of Baltimore from Cardinal Fransonius, Prefect of the Sacred Congregation of the Propaganda.[16] Commenting on the decree concerning the banns, the Cardinal said:

. . . cum cautelae loco et veluti prudentiae remedium haec bannorum publicatio haberi debeat, nulla ratio satis firma videtur obesse, quominus proclamationes, etiam quando agitur de matrimoniis mixtis, fiant; quae tamen nullo adhibito religioso ritu celebrari oportet.

The statement, it should be noted, was a very guarded one—*nulla ratio satis firma videtur obesse*—yet, it was interpreted, and subjoined in footnote to the decrees of the Council, as:[17] *Ex responso S. Congregationis. . . . Banna etiam matrimoniorum mixtorum sunt proclamanda.* This misinterpretation caused much confusion later.

The American Church had grown rapidly in the preceding decades, and, five new provinces were established just at this time. What had been declared the wish of the Council of 1846 (*optandum esse*), was soon after to be made a command. The first Plenary Council met in 1852, and placed among its decrees one which made the publication of the banns a matter of obligation (*statuunt*), the law to take effect on Easter Sunday of 1853. The decree made no distinction between Catholic and mixed marriages, and omitted the note appended in 1847.[18]

In a diocesan synod of 1853, however, Archbishop Kenrick

---

[16] The letter of July 2, 1847, contained the confirmation, and that of July 3 of the same year added the note about the banns. Both are preserved in the collection of the Provincial Councils of Baltimore—*Concilia Baltimorensia,* pp. 250-4.

[17] *Concilia Balt.,* p. 244.

[18] I Plenary Council of Balt., n. xi. (p. 46).

empowered his pastors to dispense from all publications, in a case where one party was a non-Catholic, provided that there was moral certainty of their free state.[19] The Archbishop probably did not agree with the interpretation given the letter of 1847, mentioned above, and this may have led him to inquire about it on his next visit to Rome. At any rate, he did consult the Secretary—later Prefect—of the Congregation, and was told that the letter of Cardinal Fransonius, as received at Baltimore, contained a copyist's error. Acting upon this information, the Archbishop forbade the publication of the banns before mixed marriages in his diocese.[20]

* * * * *

The action of the Baltimore Council (of 1846) renewed interest in the problem in European countries. In France, two contradictory solutions were given: in the diocese of Avignon, the banns were forbidden, whereas in Bordeaux, they were demanded.[21] The three councils in Hungary, already referred to, declared themselves in favor of publication. The Congregation of the Propaganda issued an instruction in 1862 in which it signified that missionaries were not to be prohibited from publishing the banns for marriages between Catholics and non-Catholics.[22] The most important of this group of decisions, however, is the one reached by the Council of Smyrna.[23] It laid down a rule which the Holy See applied in the subsequent American answers, and which, through them, became in substance the law of the Code. The rule established at Smyrna was this: . . . *non fiant in mixtis connubiis, nisi quando neces-*

---

[19] Synod of Balt., 1853, n. xiii.

[20] Synod of Balt., 1857, n. v.

[21] Prov. Council of Avignon, 1849, t. IV, c. viii—*Coll. Lac.*, IV, 342; Prov. Council of Bordeaux, t. III, c. viii, de mat., n. 4—*Coll. Lac.*, IV, 575. The Council of Bordeaux was probably influenced by the note in the decrees of VI Prov. Balt. (*N. R. T.*, XV [1883], 590).

[22] S. C. S. Off., litt. (ad Vic. Ap. Myssurien.), 26 Nov. 1862—*Coll. P. F.* # 1232.

[23] *Decreta Concilli Smyrnen.*, 1869, sec. ii, c. 5, *de mat.*, n. 5—*Coll. Lac.*, VI, 572.

sariae vel opportunae videantur judicio Ordinarii pro detegendis impedimentis, et omissa mentione religionis eorum, qui nuptias sint contracturi.

* * * * *

The correction made by Archbishop Kenrick caused some uncertainty in America, and in 1864, the Bishop of Natchez asked for and received an interpretation from Rome, advising him that the banns could be published.[24] Nevertheless, the Baltimore Ritual of 1866 forbade the banns without any exception, and this regulation continued through all the editions up to that of 1874, inclusive.[25] The matter was finally brought to the attention of the Holy See. The answers given are very significant.

The series of letters began with a communication to the Ordinary of Oregon City, in which was commended the course prescribed by the Natchez instruction and by the Council of Smyrna. One of the suffrigan Bishops of the province received a somewhat similar reply a few months later.[26] In the meantime, however, the Archbishop of Oregon City had written to seek a reconciliation of the new instruction with the note contained in the Ritual. The Holy See set at rest all doubts on the matter, and made it clear that the banns could be published, under certain conditions.[27] The usual restrictive clauses were appended—namely, that a dispensation be obtained from the

---

[24] S. C. S. off., instr., 11 Maii 1862—*N. R. T.*, XV [1883], 591. The *A. E. R.*, VIII [1893], 175 notes that the practice has continued and proved satisfactory. The omission of the banns had been looked upon as a favor to, rather than as a deterrent from, mixed marriages.

[25] *Excerpta ex Rituali Romano, edit. 5a, art. Modus assistendi matrimoniis mixtis*, p. 189; in the edition of 1874, the prohibition appears on p. 514, under the same article.

[26] The letter to Oregon City is given by Konings, *Compendium*, II, p. 395, under the date of Feb. 28, 1874. The answer to the Bishop of Seattle (Nesqually) may be found in the *Coll. P. F.*, # 1417.

[27] The second letter to Oregon City, Sept. 28, 1874, is also given by Konings, *loc. cit.;* there were, besides this, two letters to the Archbishop of Baltimore—the first of which, given on Sept. 24, 1874, ordered the correction of the Ritual; the second, bearing the date of January 30, 1875, denied the error alleged by Archbishop Kenrick, as noted above. These last two documents are reproduced, from the archives of the Archdiocese of Baltimore, in the *A. E. R.*, VIII [1893], 374.

impediment of mixed religion, and that no mention be made of the difference of religious belief. Besides these, another was added. The banns could be announced, if the Bishop thought them necessary for the discovery of latent impediments. This prescription seems to have been taken from the decree of the Council of Smyrna, quoted under a preceding paragraph. Reference was made to that Council in two of the letters (Oregon City, Feb. 28, and Baltimore, Sept. 24), and in the third (Oregon City, Sept. 28), the wording of the restriction is strikingly similar to that of the conciliar decree:—*posse nimirum fieri proclamationes . . . at solum quando ad detegenda, si quae sint, impedimenta, eas necessarias atque opportunas esse Ordinarius in Domino censuerit. . . .*

Strangely enough, the Seattle instruction makes no mention of the clause in question, and rather seems to take the opposite view—that the omission of the banns is to be the exception, and not the rule.[28] When it is recalled that the Seattle response was issued after the first Oregon instruction above, the Sacred Congregation itself seems to have been confused. It may be that the first letter to Oregon City, as recorded by Konings, is not authentic. He does not indicate the source from which he obtained it, and its contents are so fragmentary that doubt of its genuineness does not seem unwarranted. If this letter is rejected, the difficulty disappears—for the spirit of the Seattle letter corresponds rather to the discipline outlined in 1847, whereas the instructions given in the letters of September 1874 represent the later modification.

The importance of this correspondence lies in its interpretative value. The Ritual adopted, in substance, the directions contained in these letters,[29] and the question was closed, and

---

[28] The response itself made no reference to this condition, but in the accompanying letter, the Bishop was advised to *dispense* from publication, if he was certain of the absence of impediments. This seems to imply that the publication was obligatory until a dispensation was granted.

[29] *Rituale Romanum,* 1895: Appendix for U. S., p. 12, "Modus Assistendi Matrimoniis Mixtis": "Quoad proclamationes Bannorum, Sancta Sedes hisce postremis temporibus declaravit, illas fieri posse in mixtis nuptiis quae Apostolica dispensatione contrahuntur, suppressa tamen men-

remained so to the Code, at least as far as regards pronouncements from the Holy See. They were the latest factors in determining the discipline contained in the Code, and therefore are of the greatest value in interpreting the new legislation.

Several American synods dealt with the matter subsequently, but it seems that only two of them were acquainted with the letters of 1874.[30] Eleven other synods refused to tolerate the publication of the banns,[31] and another took the opposite stand, and favored announcing the banns before all marriages.[32]

The commentators were no more in agreement than the synods. D'Annibale thought that the banns should be omitted, while Lehmkuhl held that they could be published, if no mention was made of the difference of religion.[33] Bangen was, in principle, against the announcing of the banns, but admitted that custom made it lawful in certain places.[34] Gasparri favored omitting the announcements, although he conceded the power of contrary customs to alter this rule.[35] De Smet remarked that the general practice in England was to publish.[36] An article in the American Ecclesiastical Review reproduced the norms laid down in

---

tione Religionis conjugum: at solum quando ad detegenda si quae sint impedimenta, eas necessarias atque opportunas Ordinarius in Domino censuerit.''

30 III Synod of Newark, 1878, n. 82, c.; and I Synod of Omaha, 1887, n. 98.

31 IX Synod of Baltimore, 1886, n. 55, forbade the banns, except when they could not be omitted, owing to the civil law of Maryland, and even in that case, the publication was to take place after Mass, and without mention of the difference of religion. Prohibitions were also issued at: IV Synod of Boston, 1886, n. 139 (following the rule laid down at the II Synod, 1868, n. 121); II Synod of Richmond, 1886, c. v, de sac., n. 84; II Synod of Leavenworth, 1887, c. xxii, 2, n. 119; I Synod of Santa Fé, 1888, n. 8, 4; Synod of Fort Wayne, 1903, c. vii, n. 165; IV Synod of Louisville, 1874, c. viii, n. 6; II Synod of Dubuque, 1902, n. 103; II Synod of Davenport, 1904, n. 101; II Synod of Sioux City, 1909, n. 117, f; and II Synod of Kansas City, 1912, n. 133.

32 V Synod of Natchez, 1886, n. xli.

33 D'Annibale, *Summula Theologiae Moralis,* III, n. 465; Lehmkuhl, *Theologia Moralis,* II, n. 913.

34 *Instructio Practica,* p. 21.

35 *De Mat.,* nn. 457 and 698.

36 De Smet, *Betrothment and Marriage,* I, 54.

the letters of 1874, but regarded them as special concessions to America, on account of the unstable conditions here.[37] The only summary that can be given of the discipline before the Code is—there was no general law, and no uniformity of practice.

---

[37] *A. E. R.*, XIX [1898], 543.

PART II

THE PRESENT LEGISLATION

CHAPTER V

THE OBLIGATION TO PUBLISH THE BANNS

Canon 1022. Publice a parocho denuntietur inter quosnam matrimonium sit contrahendum.

ART. 1. THE SERIOUS NATURE OF THE OBLIGATION

It is an admitted principle of canonical jurisprudence that a law *per se* begets an obligation proportionate to the gravity of its object.[1] In view of the purpose of the banns, guarding as they do the sanctity of Christian marriage, and of the service they render in averting the spiritual and social evils of clandestinity, none can deny their importance. Almost unanimously, canonists, both before and after the Code, have regarded the publication of the banns as a serious obligation.[2] The history and the text of the law demand such an interpretation. The old law not only commanded that the banns be published, but threatened delinquents with severe canonical penalties; this certainly is undeniable evidence that the legislator wished to enforce his enactment under pain of grave sin. The present law, even though it has abrogated the sanctions,[3] reproduces the former legislation almost to the letter, and can, therefore, be regarded as accepting its legacy of severity.[4] This strict interpretation of Canon 1022 is further borne out by the Code itself

---

[1] St. Alphonsus, *Homo Apostolicus*, tr. ii, *de legibus*, c. 2, n. 14; Van Hove, *De Legibus Ecclesiasticis*, n. 136.

[2] Soto, *Comment. in IV Sent.*, d. 28, q. 1, a. 1, and Ledesma, *De Mat.*, q. 45, a. 5, held the view that the omission of the banns was not a serious offense, unless local legislation enforced the law with censures. On the other hand, some authors, cited by Sanchez, *De Mat.*, III, d. 5, n. 2, maintained that the omission of the banns would invalidate marriage: the most prominent proponent of the opinion was Menochius, *Concil.*, l. iv, c. 398.

[3] Canon 6, § 5.

[4] Canon 6, §§ 2 and 3.

in subsequent canons, which forbid pastors to give the permission to assist,[5] and which make assistance unlawful,[6] until the requirements here prescribed have been fulfilled.

The question of the quality of the sin committed by those guilty of partial infractions of the law, and other similar matters, belong more properly to the field of moral theology, and will not be treated here.

Art. 2. The Subjects of the Obligation

Indirectly, the contracting parties are subject to the obligation imposed by this law, and in two ways. They have the positive duty of informing the pastor of their matrimonial plans in time to have the publications made in all the churches required by the law. Besides this, they are bound in a negative way, namely, not to enter marriage until the banns have been announced.

Primarily and directly, the obligation of making the publications is placed upon the pastor or pastors of the parties, and also upon other pastors in certain cases.[7] This is clear from canon 1022, especially when taken in conjunction with canon 462, § 4, and from the very nature of the case; for the essence of this obligation is the making of the public announcements, a task which the parties themselves cannot perform, and which the law reserves to the pastor.

Even though he delegates some other priest to assist at the marriage, he does not thereby transfer this duty of announcing the banns, for this obligation is entirely distinct from the office of assisting at marriage. Not only is the pastor bound to make the publications, but he has also the exclusive right to do so, the proclaiming of the banns being numbered among the reserved parochial functions.[8] The pastor may permit another priest to fulfill this office for him; in fact, he may commit the task to a

---

[5] Canon 1096, § 2.

[6] Canon 1097, § 1°.

[7] What is said here of pastors applies to quasi-pastors (canon 216, § 3); to vicars endowed with full parochial powers (canons 471, 472, 474, and 475); and to the military chaplains of the United States.

[8] Canon 462, § 4.

lesser cleric, or even a layman, since the exercise of Orders or jurisdiction is not involved.[9] However, canonists hesitate to approve the practice of allowing anyone but a priest to announce proposed marriages, lest the impression be created that the banns are not sufficiently important to merit the priest's attention. Generally, there will be no difficulty, since the normal and natural procedure is that the celebrant of the Mass or the preacher makes the publication. In some extraordinary case, such as Tanquerey suggests,[10] where the vicar substitute is not familiar with the language of the people, justification might be found for allowing a layman to make the publication.

In certain European dioceses, statute or custom permits the pastor to accept a stole fee on the occasion of announcing the banns.[11] According to canon 463, § 3, this fee accrues to the pastor, even though another priest actually made the publication for him.[12] The custom does not exist in the United States.

Art. 3. The Inception of the Obligation

No doubt it has happened at times that parents, or others interested in forcing the celebration of a marriage, have arranged for the matrimonial announcements without the consent of the parties. Therefore the pastor should be on his guard against this, and should not begin the publication of the banns until he has undertaken the examination outlined in canon 1020, and has received the definite assurance of the parties themselves, that they intend to be married, and consequently request the publications.[13] For his own protection, the pastor can insist that the parties make this request in writing.

---

[9] Vlaming, *Praelectiones Juris Matrimonii*, I, 133; Knecht, *Katholisches Eherecht*, p. 172; De Smet, *Betrothment and Marriage*, I, 25; Ayrinhac, *Marriage Legislation*, p. 53.

[10] *Synopsis Theologiae Moralis*, I, n. 883.

[11] Wernz-Vidal, *Jus Canonicum*, V, n. 125; Rossi, *De Matrimonii Celebratione*, n. 13; Farrugia, *De Matrimonio*, n. 61.

[12] Ferry, *Stole Fees*, p. 53.

[13] *Rituale Romanum*, t. vii, c. 1, *de sacramento matrimonii*, n. 1; Wernz-Vidal, *Jus Canonicum*, V, n. 116; Chelodi, *Jus Matrimoniale*, n. 21; Blat, *Commentarium Textus Codicis*, III, i, 514; Noldin, *Summa Theologiae Moralis*, III, n. 556.

The burden of the investigation into the free state of the parties rests principally on that proper pastor who is to witness the marriage, and it is to him that the other pastors in the case must report the results of their personal investigations.[14] If the marriage is to take place outside of the proper parishes of either party, or before a priest who is not the proper pastor of one of them, then the proper pastor who gave the license to assist, or the delegation, is the one who must conduct the private investigation.[15] Upon the completion of his own examination, and the receipt of reports from the other pastors, if any others cooperated, the pastor in charge of this investigation has the duty not only to publish the banns himself,[16] but also to notify all the other pastors who will have to make the publications according to canon 1022, and to send the Ordinary a request for instructions in those cases comprehended under canons 1023, § 2, 1031, and 1032.[17] The obligation of publishing the banns does not begin for these other pastors until they receive the request to do so from the pastor who has conducted the investigation. If, however, it becomes apparent that that pastor has neglected his duty without warrant, they may and must proceed to make the announcements.

If, after his examination of the parties, the pastor suspects the presence of an impediment, or if an impediment is reported to him, the existence of which is not certain, the pastor is obliged to pursue a more diligent and searching investigation. He may, however, commence the publications, or continue them, if they have already been begun.[18]

---

[14] Canon 1029.

[15] Benedictus XIV, ep. encycl. "Etsi minime," 7 Feb. 1742, n. 14—*Fontes* # 324; also, ep. encycl. "Nimiam licentiam," 18 Maii 1743, n. 10—*Fontes* # 337; Wernz-Vidal, *Jus Canonicum*, V, n. 116; Blat, *Commentarium Textus*, III, i, 514; De Smet, *Betrothment and Marriage*, I, 35. The proper pastor is chosen because he is presumed to be acquainted with the parties, or at least in a better position to investigate their status.

[16] Unless a public impediment has been discovered—canon 1031, § 2, 2°.

[17] Under canon 1032 are included not only *vagi*, but also emigrants from distant countries, even though they are not *vagi*. Decree of the Sacred Congregation of the Sacraments, July 4, 1921, n. 4—*A. A. S.* XIII [1921], 348.

[18] Canon 1031, § 1, 1° et 2°.

When the impediment brought to the pastor's attention is known with certainty to exist, the pastor's course of action will be determined by the circumstances. If the impediment is one which cannot be dispensed, matrimonial preparations are at an end. If the impediment is dispensable and occult, the pastor is permitted to begin or continue the publications.[19] If the impediment is public, the pastor may not commence the publications until a dispensation from the impediment has been obtained in the external forum, or at least in the internal non-sacramental forum. However, if the publications had been begun before the discovery of the impediment, the pastor is permitted to make the remaining one or two announcements.[20]

In what sense are the words *publicum* and *occultum* to be taken in this canon? Are they to be construed according to the definition given in canon 1037, under which an impediment is public, when it can be proved in the external forum, by sufficient testimony, or other acceptable proof? It seems not.

An analysis of the reasons apparently behind the distinction of public and occult impediments in canon 1031, § 2 leads one to conclude that the terms are here to be understood in relation to the knowledge or ignorance of the community about the existence of the impediment.

When the law provides that the pastor may begin or continue the publications after discovering an occult impediment, it is evidently seeking to protect the good name of the parties laboring under the impediment, and to avert the general suspicion the postponement of the banns might cause. When, on the other hand, it forbids the pastor to begin publication, if he has already discovered a public impediment, the purpose is, evidently, to avoid the scandal such action would provoke. Now, the scandal in view is the scandal of the community; for, if the term "public" were accepted in the strict sense of canon 1037, and two persons knew of the impediment, that impediment would be public, and the banns postponed to avoid scandalizing those persons; but such scandal could easily be removed. Moreover, if only one person knew of the impediment, or if one of those

[19] Canon 1031, § 2, 1°.

[20] Canon 1031, § 2, 2°.

two who did know was excluded from testifying[21] (waiving the question of the probative value of documents and the judicial confession of the parties), the impediment would be secret, and the pastor would be allowed to publish the banns, without considering the scandal suffered by those people. It would be unreasonable to suppose that the legislator intended the law to be interpreted in such a way as to make its application ridiculous. The conclusion can therefore be safely drawn that the pastor is forbidden to begin the publication of the banns only when there is present an impediment which is known to several persons in the parish.[22]

---

[21] Canon 1757.

[22] Blat, *Commentarium Textus,* III, i, 526. The opposite opinion is upheld by Augustine, *Commentary,* V, 76. None of the other available authors treats the question.

CHAPTER VI

THE FORM OF THE PUBLICATIONS

The Code gives only a very meagre outline of the form in which the matrimonial publications are to be made. Regarding the general characteristics of these announcements, the law first proposes the traditional oral method, and besides, extends to the whole Church permission to use the written mode, as an alternative.

The legislator emphasizes only one quality in the publications. Whether in written or oral form, the banns must be publicly announced.[1] The word "public" is here to be taken in its natural etymological sense, and not in the restricted meaning given the word elsewhere in the matrimonial legislation.[2] Hence, the announcements must be made in such a way that the information contained in them can easily become known to all the parishioners. If the publication is given orally, it must be sufficiently loud and distinct to be intelligible to the congregation; if the names are published by a written notice, that must be posted in a conspicuous place in the church, at or near the entrance. In both cases, the vernacular language of the locality must be employed.

Art. 1. The Details to be Announced

The Code indicates the contents of the announcements only in a very general way, using the phrases *inter quosnam matrimonium sit contrahendum* (canon 1022), and *affixionem nominum contrahentium* (canon 1025). The Ritual, on the other hand, presents a very complete formula,[3] but does not enforce

[1] Canon 1022—*publice denuntietur;* canon 1025—*publicam . . . affixionem.*

[2] Canon 1037.

[3] "Notum sit omnibus hic praesentibus, quod N., filius N., familiae N., paroeciae S. N., et N., filia N., familiae N., paroeciae S. N., intendunt inter se contrahere Matrimonium. Proinde admonemus omnes et singulos, ut si

its use to the exclusion of other forms introduced by usage or local law.[4]

The necessary content of the announcements can be determined from a study of the purpose of the banns. The entire legislation is intended to urge the cooperation of the faithful in reporting impediments to a proposed marriage, if any impediments are known to exist. To achieve this purpose, it is necessary that the publications contain information sufficient for the identification of the parties, that they inculcate the obligation incumbent on the faithful of revealing impediments, and that they indicate the time available for making these reports. An announcement so constructed fully satisfies the mandates of the Code, and contains all the elements indicated in the Ritual model.

The details needed for a certain and unmistakable identification will vary according to the size of the community and the prominence of the person. In a rural parish, the name of a local parishioner will generally be enough to enable the people to identify him beyond any doubt; the full name of the other party should be given, and in addition the parish and town of residence. In populous areas, a more detailed description will have to be given, lest the people fail to recognize, or confuse the party with others of similar name. The pastor of a city or suburban parish should therefore make it a practice to include in his announcements the address, at least of that one of the parties who lives in his parish. An objection may be raised, that the Ritual demands no more than the mention of the parochial affiliation of the parties, and that the addition of the address is an unjustified innovation. Several of the more recent

---

quis noverit aliquod consanguinitatis, vel affinitatis, vel cognationis spiritualis, vel quodvis aliud impedimentum inter eos esse, quod Matrimonium contrahendum invicem impediat, illud quamprimum Parocho aut loci Ordinario revelare debeat; et hoc admonemus primo (si sit prima), vel secundo (si sit secunda), vel tertio (si sit tertia publicatio).'' *Rituale Romanum*, t. vii, c. 1, *de sacramento matrimonii*, n. 8.

[4] Wernz-Vidal, *Jus Canonicum*, V, n. 128; Cappello, *De Sacramentis*, III, n. 167; Prümmer, *Manuale Theologiae Moralis*, III, 737; Cerato, *Matrimonium*, p. 33.

authors, however, look upon it as a very necessary addition.[5] Whether the Ritual contains any prescription on the matter, or not, is entirely beside the question. The Code itself obliges the pastor to add this information; for, in order to properly fulfill the precept of the banns, he must make his announcements in such a manner that the people can recognize the parties concerned; therefore, he must include all facts which are required for a complete identification. That address is, in the great majority of cases, a very necessary factor in the process of identification, few will deny.

The Roman Ritual and many of the old diocesan rituals indicate that the names of the parents of both parties should be mentioned. Here it must be recalled, that the Roman Ritual does not demand strict, word for word adherence to the formula it describes; the form is given only as a model.[6] Priests in dioceses which have their own local customary or statutory formulae will have to be guided by the prescriptions contained therein. But apart from such particular regulations, it is difficult to establish the existence of any obligation or necessity to add this detail in all cases. Its presence in the Ritual formula is easily explained: the mention of the parents' names may at times become necessary for identifying the parties, as for instance, when there are several families of the same name living in the same vicinity: the Ritual, therefore, offers a formula complete enough to suggest this extra point of identification to the pastor, without obliging him to use it in cases where it is unnecessary. In the average announcement, the mention of the parents' names serves little useful purpose, and may at times lead to a very embarrassing situation, that is, when one of the parties is illegitimate.

Besides the information necessary for the identification of the parties, two other items must be included in the publications.

---

[5] De Smet, *Betrothment and Marriage,* I, 30; Rossi, *De Matrimonii Celebratione,* n. 16; Fourneret, *Le Mariage Chrétien,* p. 107; Vlaming, *Praelectiones Juris Matrim.,* I, 132, who refers to the Synod of Haarlem, 1919, p. 3, as requiring it.

[6] Cappello, *De Sacramentis,* III, n. 167; Fourneret, *Le Mariage Chrétien,* p. 107.

First, the congregation must be admonished about the duty imposed on those who have definite knowledge of an impediment or any other obstacle—such as a defect of consent—to the valid and lawful celebration of the marriage. Then, in order that these people may not delay too long in making their reports, some indication must be given them as to the amount of time at their disposal. Generally, this is done by distinguishing the first, second, and third publication; that method involves the difficulty, though, that the congregation must be informed, whenever a dispensation from one or two publications has been given. It would probably serve the purpose much better to announce the date of the marriage, unless the parties have some valid objection to that.

Art. 2. The Details to be Omitted

Some canonists[7] state that, when one or both of the parties has been previously married, that circumstance should be contained in the announcements. Perhaps it is necessary at times, in order to identify a widow, to give both her maiden name, and her deceased husband's name in that case; the former marriage must be alluded to. Outside of such an instance, it seems advisable to omit all mention of a previous marriage. The contrary practice involves all sorts of difficulties. Some marriages are not terminated by death; some unions terminated by death, and commonly thought to be marriages, were never more than mere concubinage. It would be very difficult for the priest to explain these cases to people unfamiliar with the law. Furthermore, the reference to the previous marriage will contribute nothing to the effectiveness of the banns; if any of the faithful doubt the freedom of the parties, they will probably reveal their suspicions anyway; if they do not entertain any doubts on the matter, why inform them of the previous marriage?

It has also been suggested[8] that the pastor make mention of

[7] De Smet, *Betrothment and Marriage,* I, 30; Augustine, *Commentary on Canon Law,* V, 57; Tanquerey, *Synopsis Theologiae Moralis,* I, n. 888; Joder, *Formulaire Matrimonial,* p. 32.

[8] De Smet, *Betrothment and Marriage,* I, 30.

any public impediments from which the parties have been dispensed. The prudence of such a practice seems questionable. The basis for the suggestion is, of course, that the people will be prone to presume that the priest shares in the public knowledge of the impediment, and has already procured the dispensation, unless they know that he is in the habit of informing them of all public impediments of which he is cognizant. But there surely is no reason why the priest should cater to such unfounded presumptions on the part of the people. They should be instructed to report all impediments, even those publicly known. Informing the whole congregation about the private affairs of the couple about to be married will certainly embarrass them. No matter whether the impediment in the case reflects on the character of the parties, or does not, the very fact that a dispensation was necessary is enough to cause comment, unjustified though it be, and to attach a certain amount of reproach to a perfectly lawful marriage.

It is quite significant that the Ritual, so complete with regard to other details, makes no reference to any need or obligation to mention the previous marriages of the parties, or the public impediments from which they have been dispensed.

Facts such as the age and occupation of the parties should likewise be omitted, and mention should never be made of any other circumstance which would cause the parties discomfort, or, worse still, defamation.

CHAPTER VII

THE PARISHES IN WHICH THE PUBLICATIONS MUST BE MADE

The publication of the banns is always a matter of obligation for the proper pastor of each party, and at times, becomes the duty of other pastors as well.

Art. 1. The Obligation of Proper Pastors

Canon 1023, § 1. Matrimoniorum publicationes fieri debent a proprio parocho.

The matrimonial publications are part of the process of determining the freedom of the parties, and as such are especially addressed to their friends and acquaintances. The average person is best known in the neighborhood of his home; there more people know him than anywhere else, and their knowledge, of his social status at least, is more accurate and intimate. The Church takes advantage of this neighborly interest, and lays down as the primary principle of publication, that the proper pastor of each party is to make the announcements.

The Code uses the singular number, and speaks of the *proprio parocho,* but it does not thereby limit the duty to one pastor, if the parties in the case have several pastors. Announcing the banns at the church in which the wedding is to take place does not always fully satisfy the provisions of the law. Such a restricted interpretation is excluded by the text of the law, which, in using the singular form, imposes the obligation individually on each of those priests qualified as the proper pastors of the parties.

Parochial affiliation is to be determined by the factors enumerated in canons 93 and 94—namely, domicile, quasi-domicile, legal domicile, or, in the case of *vagi,* and of those who have only a diocesan domicile, actual residence within the parish limits.

a. *Parish of Domicile or Quasi-Domicile.*

Even though a person has only recently established his domicile or quasi-domicile in a parish, the pastor of that place is bound to make the publications.[1] Formerly, there was a great deal of confusion on the interpretation of this point of the law. In many dioceses the practice prevailed of not publishing the banns in a newly acquired domicile until two months of residence had been completed there.[2] The Code, however, makes no distinction about the length of tenure of one's domicile, but simply obliges the pastors of the places of domicile or quasi-domicile to publish the banns; the old practice must, therefore, be abolished, unless it can enjoy the protection afforded by canon 5. Generally the banns will be useless in such cases because the parties are not sufficiently well known in their new parishes, but that fact will not in itself justify the pastor in omitting the publications. Appeal to the mind of the legislator or to the purpose of the law is out of the question, for that recourse is open only when the precise meaning of the law is doubtful. Which is not the case here. *Epikeia* might be suggested, but at best that is a treacherous remedy, and considering the importance of the banns, in contrast with the little labor involved in making the publications, such use of *epikeia* seems unreasonable and entirely out of order. The only avenue of escape from this seemingly useless obligation is through dispensation.

Epikeia may be admissible, however, in a case where one of the parties changes his or her residence after the publications have already been commenced. First of all, it is always open

---

[1] After the promulgation of the decree "Ne Temere," some of the leading canonists—Wernz, *Jus Decretalium,* IV, 184; Vermeersch, *De Forma Sponsalium et Matrimonii post Decretum "Ne Temere,"* n. 65;—questioned the necessity of publishing the banns in the parish of quasi-domicile. They contended that the month's residence had displaced it in all parts of the matrimonial law. Whatever value the opinion had during the decade the decree was in effect, the Code has now divested it of all remnant of probability.

[2] This was the custom in Rome. Wernz, *Jus Decretalium,* IV, 187. In the province of Albi, the period was set at six months: Prov. Council of Albi, 1850, *T. V., decr.* ix, *n.* 3—*Coll. Lac.,* IV, 435.

to question whether this new residence is really a domicile or quasi-domicile—whether the party means to establish it independently of the outcome of the contemplated marriage.[3] But, even supposing that a true domicile or quasi-domicile is established, it seems that insistence on the letter of the law in this case would push the obligation to ridiculous extremes. It is probably lawful to appeal to *epikeia*.

b. *Parish of Legal Domicile*

Three classes of persons are accorded legal or necessary domiciles in canon law—minors; married women, unless legitimately separated from their husbands; and the insane. In this treatise, discussion can be limited to the first group.[4]

In the case of minor children, the banns must be published in the parish where the parental domicile[5] is located, even though the minor no longer resides there.[6] The observance of this

---

[3] S. C. C., *in causa Parisien.*, 20 Aug. 1898—*Anal. Eccl.* VII [1899], 73; S. R. Rota, *in causa Parisien.*, 5 Maii 1914—*A. A. S.*, VI [1914], 397.

[4] About the insane there is no difficulty; they are excluded from marriage. As regards a married woman who makes use of the Pauline Privilege, the strict letter of the law would seem to oblige the pastor of the parish where the first husband retains a domicile, to publish the banns for the second marriage, unless the woman had been legitimately separated according to the norms of canon 1131, § 1, and the decision of the Pontifical Commission for the Interpretation of the Canons of the Code, July 22, 1922—*A. A. S.*, XIV [1922], 526. But the legislator can hardly be regarded as insisting on this rigorous interpretation; it seems admissable, therefore, to invoke *epikeia*, especially if the woman has never lived in the husband's present domicile. At any rate, canon 1023, §§ 2 and 3, will be applicable in most cases, and will provide sufficient safeguard for the second marriage.

[5] If the parents have no domicile, but only a quasi-domicile, there is no obligation to publish the banns in that place. Canonists are not in agreement as to the existence of a legal quasi-domicile in the new legislation, and therefore no certain obligation to publish the banns in the parental quasi-domicile can be established. On the question of the legal quasi-domicile, consult Costello, *Domicile and Quasi Domicile*, pp. 174-177.

[6] This duty urges even when both parents are infidels, first because the legal domicile is given to the baptized child, who is certainly capable of a canonical domicile, and secondly, because even the infidel parents are regarded as able to acquire a domicile under canon law: cfr. Schenk,

prescription of the law prevents the celebration of a marriage without the knowledge of the parents of the minor, and increases the possibility of discovering long latent impediments, impediments known perhaps only to the old friends and neighbors of the family.

After the person attains his or her majority, the legal domicile ceases, and consequently the obligation of publishing the banns there, unless that domicile is then retained as a voluntary domicile. Mere absence does not suffice to indicate that the party has surrendered this parental domicile; the two necessary elements—departure, coupled with the intention of not returning—must be present, and not only present, but clearly made manifest, since the loss of domicile is not to be presumed.[7]

c. *Parish of Actual Residence*

Residence, taken here as distinct from parochial domicile or quasi-domicile, must also be considered as a factor in determining the obligation of the banns. Persons who have only a diocesan domicile, and those who have no domicile or quasi-domicile anywhere—*vagi*—are members of the parish in which they are actually staying. This residence makes them subject to the pastor of that parish, and obliges him to publish the banns before their marriages.

Some canonists would oblige the pastor to publish the banns for the marriages of those *peregrini* who have established a month's residence in his parish, and intend to be married there.[8] These commentators maintain that the publication of the banns

---

Mixed Religion and Disparity of Cult, p. 284; Kay, *Competence in Matrimonial Procedure*, p. 74; *Votum Consultoris* in the decision of the Sacred Congregation of the Sacraments. Dec. 14, 1915—*A. A. S.* VIII [1916], 66.

[7] S. R. Rota, *in causa Parisien.*, 24 Mart. 1911—*A. A. S.* III [1911], 326; S. R. Rota, *in causa Parisien.*, 27 Jan. 1912—*A. A. S.* IV [1912], 282; S. R. Rota, *in causa Gratianopolitana*, 17 Jul. 1912—*A. A. S.* IV [1912], 677; S. R. Rota, *in causa Ravennaten.*, 8 Apr. 1913—*A. A. S.* V [1913], 340; S. R. Rota, *in causa Parisien.*, 5 Maii 1914—*A. A. S.* VI [1914], 397.

[8] Blat, *Commentarium Textus*, III, i, 518; Rossi, *De Matrimonii Celebratione*, p. 13; Fanfani, *De Jure Parochorum*, p. 281.

is a necessary means of attaining the assurance of free state demanded of the pastor who is to assist at a marriage.[9]

A pastor who would make it a practice to publish all such marriages would undoubtedly merit great praise for his zeal, but it is difficult to see how he could be obliged to do it by virtue of canon 1020, § 1. The Code carefully distinguishes between the parochial investigation and the publications,[10] and gives no indication of including the publication of the banns under the investigation commanded in canon 1020, § 1.

d. *National Parishes*

In practically every American diocese there are several parishes particularly devoted to the people of a certain nationality or race.[11] These parishes are only remotely limited by territory; they are generally constituted for all the people of a particular nationality or race living within the limits of a town, district or city.[12] The pastors of these parishes are, in a wide sense, personal pastors; the membership of their parish is determined, not by residence or domicile, but by national origin and descent.[13] Their parishioners are, by a fiction of law, removed from the jurisdiction of the territorial pastor of the parish in which they live,[14] and have as their one and only proper pastor, the pastor of the national parish. Therefore that pastor has

[9] Canons 1020, § 1 and 1097, § 1, 1°.

[10] Canons 1029 and 1030, § 1.

[11] Reference is here made to parishes of the Latin rite. The Oriental law on the banns is treated elsewhere. In the case of a marriage between a Latin Catholic and an Oriental Catholic, the banns must be published in the parish or parishes of the Latin party; Oriental pastors will be guided by their own law.

[12] At times the restriction is placed that only those who have actually emigrated from the particular country in Europe, and the first generation of their descendants may become members of the national parish.

[13] De Smet, *Betrothment and Marriage*, I, 71; Wernz-Vidal, *Jus Canonicum*, V, n. 535.

[14] The territorial pastor may validly assist at the marriages of subjects of national pastors, but needs permission to assist lawfully, even though the party has a domicile in his parish. S. C. C., 1 Feb. 1908, ad 8—*A. S.*, XLI [1908], 65. Cfr. also De Smet, *loc. cit.*

the duty of publishing the banns rather than the territorial pastor.

These people may give up their membership in the national parish, and subject themselves to the regular territorial pastor. In that case the obligation of announcing the banns reverts to the pastor of the parish in which they have their domicile, quasi-domicile or residence.

ART. 2. THE OBLIGATION OF OTHER PASTORS

Canon 1023, § 2. Si pars alio in loco per sex menses commorata sit post adeptam pubertatem, parochus rem exponat Ordinario, qui pro sua prudentia vel publicationes inibi faciendas exigat, vel alias probationes seu conjecturas super status libertatae colligendas praescribat.

The general law has never made it obligatory to publish the banns in any of the previous residences of the parties. The Holy See, it is true, has counseled the publication of the banns in the former residences,[15] and local laws have often made this course compulsory, but the common law has always allowed the alternative of using other forms of inquiry. The Code continues this policy.

According to the present law, if one or both parties resided outside the parish, which, at the time of marriage, is his or her proper parish, and continued that residence for the period of six months after attaining puberty, the pastor in charge of the investigation is obliged to notify the Bishop, even though he is certain that no impediment was contracted during that time.

The Ordinary is then empowered to pursue either of two methods. He can, if he so chooses, order the publication of the banns. This is the better procedure when the residence in that other place has been terminated only a short time previously.[16] It must be borne in mind, though, that the Ordinary can issue

---

[15] Thus, the Instruction of the Holy Office, Aug. 22, 1890—*A. S.*, XXIII [1890], 189.

[16] Rossi, *De Matrimonii Celebratione*, n. 13. Thus, the new statutes of Paris, n. 157,—*Statuts Synodaux*, p. 45.

a strict command to publish the banns only to the pastors within the limits of his own territory; elsewhere, he may request that the publications be made, and his wishes should be respected, since it may be presumed that he has good reason for asking this maximum of precaution in a given case.

Instead of the banns, the Ordinary may prescribe that the pastor who is directing the investigation seek other proofs and indications of the free state of the parties. What these are to be the law does not say. The oaths of the parties are admissible, but only as a last resort.[17] The most reliable evidence would be a testimonial letter from the pastor of the parish in which the former residence was located, if he was acquainted with the parties, and next in value to that, the attestation of reliable persons, who lived in that other place and knew the parties. Civil documents which purport to certify the party's freedom are of little value, since the civil law recognizes few of the ecclesiastical impediments, and generally accepts divorce as an effective terminant of the marriage bond. The high moral character of the parties themselves would be sufficient to establish at least a conjecture in their favor. In any case, the total of proof must yield moral certainty, in order to fulfill the requirements of canons 1019, § 1, and 1097, § 1, 1°.

It is not at all necessary for the residence in question to have been in another diocese. According to the strict letter of the canon, the pastor would be obliged to consult the Bishop even if this residence had been in an adjacent parish.[18]

This residence elsewhere ordinarily must have been protracted

---

[17] This is evident from a comparison of canons 1019, § 2, 1031, § 1, 1830, § 1, and especially from the response of the Pontifical Commission, June 2-3, 1918, ad 4.—*A. A. S.*, X [1918], 345. Cfr. also *Jus Pontificium,* I [1921], 25.

[18] De Smet, *Betrothment and Marriage,* I, 29; Prümmer, *Manuale Theologiae Moralis,* n. 738; Farrugia, *De Matrimonio,* n. 62, 2; Augustine, *Commentary,* V, 59. Ubach, *Compendium Theologiae Moralis,* II, 418, suggests that the term "alio in loco" was used in the canon instead of "paroecia," in order to include residence in those regions where parishes have not yet been erected. In all probability, the term can be traced to the instruction from the Holy Office, Aug. 22, 1890, in which a similar expression was used.

for six months. Not that there is any intrinsic reason why six months should be the norm; an impediment could certainly be contracted in a much shorter space of time; the legislator, in fact, explicitly states that the Ordinary can insist on the added inquiry even when the residence did not extend through six months; but, this period is generally accepted as the minimum time in which there would be the likelihood of a canonical impediment arising.[19]

The canon does not give any definite indication as to whether a series of interrupted visits totaling six months in a particular place would give rise to the same obligation. In view of the next section of the same canon, it seems safe to conclude that the legislator intended this prescription to refer only to a continuous stay.[20]

No matter how long the party has lived in his present domicile, as long as he spent six months elsewhere at any time after attaining the age of puberty, the pastor who is conducting the principal investigation must notify the Ordinary of this fact. Absence before puberty is not considered in this matter. Some authors[21] reckon puberty according to the standards of canon 1067, arguing that the legislator meant to continue the former discipline, which dated this recourse as from the time the parties attained marriageable age.[22] They would now compute the duty imposed in canon 1023, § 2 from the sixteenth year for the man, and the fourteenth year for the woman. Everything, however, argues against such a stand, and in favor of accepting natural puberty—fourteen and twelve years of age respectively—as the gauge of this obligation. First of all, the legislator does not give any hint that he wishes to alter the meaning of "puberty" as previously defined in canon 88. Furthermore, appeal to the old discipline in every way confirms the stricter interpretation: for marriageable age under the old law differed from its present definition in canon 1067, and corresponded to the presumed time

---

[19] Cfr. canons 999, § 4 and 994.

[20] Blat, *Commentarium Textus,* III, i, 518.

[21] Augustine, *Commentary,* V, 59; Petrovits, *New Church Law on Matrimony,* p. 50.

[22] Instruction of the Holy Office, Aug. 22, 1890—*A. S.*, XXIII [1890], 189.

of natural puberty determined by canon 88. Then too, the legislator undoubtedly had the Holy Office instruction of 1890 in mind when formulating this canon, and yet deliberately chose the term "puberty," instead of "marriageable age," as contained in that instruction. The overwhelming majority of canonists favor this strict view.[23]

This section of canon 1023, if it were faithfully observed, would place a very heavy burden on the Ordinary. It is safe to say that the great majority of marriages, especially in the United States, fall under the prescriptions of canon 1023, § 2. In most instances, the freedom of the parties will be evident to the pastor after his investigation, and recourse to the Ordinary will be superfluous. Yet the canon dictates that each case be presented to the Ordinary for his consideration.

The difficulty involved in the observance of this canon was soon perceived, and authors[24] suggested that Ordinaries incorporate in their diocesan statutes a general regulation, which would transfer this obligation from the Bishop to the pastors, and enable the latter to conduct and conclude their investigations without consulting the Bishop. Cases involving immigrants, however, and such similar cases which present special problems in the conducting of the examination, must be reserved to the Ordinary.[25]

This policy has been adopted already in certain European dioceses.[26]

The Bishop may consign the consideration of even the more difficult cases, which have been reserved to himself, to another

---

[23] Vlaming, *Praelectiones Juris Matr.*, I, 140; *Cappello, De Sacramentis,* III, n. 164, 4; Vermeersch-Creusen, *Epitome,* II, n. 289; Blat, *Commentarium Textus,* III, i, 518; Fanfani, *De Jure Parochorum,* p. 277.

[24] Vlaming, *Praelectiones Juris Matrimonii,* I, 141; Chelodi, *Jus Matrimoniale,* n. 25; De Smet, *Betrothment and Marriage,* I, 29; Vermeersch-Creusen, *Epitome,* II, n. 289; Wernz-Vidal, *Jus Canonicum,* V, n. 124; Augustine, *Commentary,* V, 58.

[25] S. C. de Sacramentis, instr., 4 Julii 1921, ad 4.—*A. A. S.*, XIII [1921], 348-9.

[26] Thus, in Mechlin, IV Provincial Council, 1920, n. 206—Vermeersch-Creusen, *Epitome,* II, n. 289; also in Harlem, Synod of 1919, n. 6—Vlaming, *Praelectiones Juris Matrimonii,* I, 142.

priest,—the Chancellor, for example. For, although the law commits the matter to the Ordinary's prudence, he is not thereby chosen *industria personae,* but may appoint another to discharge this office for him.[27]

ART. 3. THE OBLIGATION IN SPECIAL CASES

Canon 1023, § 3. Si aliqua sit suspicio de contracto impedimento, parochus etiam pro breviore commoratione consulat Ordinarium, qui matrimonium ne permittat, nisi prius suspicio, ad normam § 2, removeatur.

This section of the canon empowers the Ordinary to command a special investigation of the parties, or the publication of the banns, even though they did not spend six months outside their present domiciles. The legislator indicates that this is an extraordinary precaution, necessary only when the existence of an impediment is suspected.

The suspicion should concern the person's conduct during the period of residence outside his present domicile. Otherwise, there would be no reason for obliging the pastor to have recourse to the Ordinary, at least immediately; for, canon 1031, § 1, 1°. allows the pastor to conduct the investigation of any doubt that arises in ordinary cases, and imposes the obligation of consulting the Ordinary only when the means at the pastor's command have failed to resolve the doubt.

Whether the Ordinary can go still further, and oblige his pastors to consult him, even when there is no suspicion against the party, and his residence elsewhere was not protracted for six months, is a matter open to question. Rossi[28] and Cappello[29] deny him the power to enforce the publication of the banns. This is probably true; at least, there is nothing in the law which could be adduced to prove the Bishop's right to insist on the

---

[27] A power which is given to all Ordinaries, even though it is committed to their prudence, cannot be regarded as accorded them *industria personae.* Schmalzgrueber, *Jus Eccl.,* IV, iii, n. 30.

[28] *De Matrimonii Celebratione,* n. 13.

[29] *De Sacramentis,* III, n. 164, 4.

publications. But, it seems certain that he can command a special investigation in any case,[30] and can ordain by general statute that pastors consult him before assisting at the marriages of certain classes of people, as for example, soldiers.[31]

In certain dioceses of Portugal, the banns are published in two parishes, even though the parties never lived outside their present domicile. This extra obligation was introduced by custom, and remains in effect even after the promulgation of the new Code, as a custom *praeter jus*.[32]

---

[30] Canon 1020, § 3.

[31] By analogy with canon 994, § 1. Several authorities place soldiers in a special category, and maintain that the banns must be published in the domicile which these men had at the time of their enlistment. Thus, Ferreres, *Compendium Theologiae Moralis,* II, 553 (8. ed., 1918); Lehmkuhl, *Theologia Moralis,* II, n. 863; Cappello, *De Sacramentis,* III, n. 164, 9. Cfr. also *Palestra del Clero,* XXXIV [1929], 408—as cited in *Jus Pontificium,* IX [1930], 203.

[32] Maia, *Direito Eclesiastico,* I [1925], 4—as cited in *Apollinaris,* II [1929], 336.

CHAPTER VIII

THE CIRCUMSTANCES OF PUBLICATION

After determining the various parishes in which the banns must be published, the Code proceeds to describe the circumstances of time and place under which the announcements are to be made. These differ, according as the oral or written method of publication is adopted.

ART. 1. ORAL PUBLICATION

Canon 1024. Publicationes fiant tribus continuis diebus dominicis aliisque festis de praecepto in ecclesia inter Missarum solemnia, aut inter alia divina officia ad quae populus frequens accedat.

Before the Code, canonists were sharply divided on the interpretation of this section, because of the tendency of some of them to depart from the letter of the Tridentine law. No doubt, these authors had good reason for their suggested modifications, but the practice led relentlessly to confusion. The Code has gone far to unravel this tangle of opinions, by adopting some of the suggested changes into the text of the law, and by definitely rejecting others.

a. *Publication on Feast Days of Precept*

The law provides that the publications must be made on three distinct Sundays, or other feasts of precept. Canon 1247, § 1 enumerates the feasts which are of universal precept; besides these, the local Ordinary is given the power to designate other days as particular feasts of precept.[1] The banns can be pub-

[1] Canon 1244, § 2. He can establish these feasts only *per modum actus*—not *in perpetuum*.

lished on any feast of obligation, whether universal or particular.[2]

The Code insists on limiting the publications to these days, because only then is the attendance of the faithful guaranteed. Under the old legislation, many authors[3] maintained that the Bishop could, even by general statute, permit the publication of the banns on feast days of mere devotion, provided that there was a sufficiently large gathering of the faithful in the church.[4] The opinion is untenable under the present legislation. The Code expressly demands that the days chosen for publication be feasts of precept. This precise determination did not exist in the text of the old law, and was added in the face of the divergent views of the pre-Code commentators. The only possible conclusion, then, is that the legislator fully intended to restrict the banns to feast days of obligation.[5]

The Bishop, it is true, may still dispense with this circumstance of the law, but the power is restricted; the dispensation can be given only in particular cases, when there is sufficient cause to warrant the departure from the law, and always on the supposition that there will be a large gathering of the parishioners present when the publication is made.[6] This last requirement is seldom verified on devotional feasts.

---

[2] Cheloidi, *Jus Matrimoniale*, n. 21; Vermeersch-Creusen, *Epitome*, II, n. 290; Blat, *Commentarium Textus*, III, i, 518; Cerato, *Matrimonium*, p. 32.

[3] St. Alphonsus, *Theologia Moralis*, VI, n. 992; D'Annibale, *Summula Theologiae Moralis*, III, n. 453; Lehmkuhl, *Theologia Moralis*, II, n. 862; Gasparri, *De Matrimonio*, n. 166.

[4] Authors understand by this term, a gathering approximately as large as that at the principal Mass on Sunday.

[5] If in any place, it had been a centenary or immemorial practice to publish the banns on feast days of mere devotion, and the Ordinary deems it imprudent to attempt to suppress the custom, that custom may be tolerated by the Ordinary—(canon 5).

[6] Vlaming, *Praelectiones Juris Matrimonii*, I, 135; Rossi, *De Matrimonii Celebratione*, n. 15; De Smet, *Betrothment and Marriage*, I, 30; Cappello, *De Sacramentis*, III, n. 165, 3. Authors attribute this power to the Bishop on the strength of the principle: "Plus semper in se continet, quod est minus"; that is, since the Bishop has power to dispense from the publications, he can dispense from the solemnities thereof.

The banns cannot be published on the four general feasts of precept[7] suppressed in this country. First, in point of fact, the attendance at Mass and other sacred functions on these days is seldom large enough to justify publication. But apart from that, even granting that there is a large number of the faithful present, these days are not actually feasts of precept in the United States, and therefore fail to come under the provisions of canon 1024.[8] Appeal would have to be made to the Bishop, in individual cases, to permit a publication to be made on one of these feasts.

b. *Publication on Three Feasts in Immediate Succession*

The Code has retained the prescription specifying that the three days chosen for publication must follow each other in a sequence unbroken on the calendar of feasts of precept. The purpose of this provision is, to prevent the undue protraction of matrimonial preparations, and to encourage the faithful to be prompt in reporting any impediments that exist. The pastor, then, must take advantage of each Sunday and feast of precept, even one established by the Ordinary according to canon 1244, § 2, unless custom,[9] or the law of a particular Council, whose acts have received the confirmation of the Holy See, regulates otherwise.

Previous to the Code, authors used to question the legality of utilizing three days which came in immediate succession, not only according to the calendar of feasts of precept, but also on the civil calendar, as for example the first three days of Easter week. Now it is impossible to have such a series of feasts, except in the rare instance where an Ordinary decrees an extraordinary

---

[7] Epiphany, St. Joseph, Corpus Christi, and Sts. Peter and Paul.

[8] Cappello, *De Sacramentis,* III, n. 165; Chelodi, *Jus Matrimoniale,* n. 26.

[9] Thus, in many dioceses there is an immemorial custom of omitting the banns on Christmas, or in Lent. Rossi, *De Matrimonii Celebratione,* n. 15; Cappello, *De Sacramentis,* III, n. 165, 3. Such customs, since they are contrary to the law, are subject to the provisions of canon 5. Cerato, *Matrimonium,* p. 33, holds that the banns may be omitted on feast days of precept falling on a week day, without breaking the prescribed continuity; he does not seek to support this assertion, merely advancing it as a statement of his own opinion.

feast of precept immediately succeeding two such feasts on the universal ecclesiastical calendar. Vlaming[10] asserts that in such a case, the pastor is obliged to postpone one of the announcements to a subsequent feast of precept. This course can hardly be described as obligatory, but it is certainly permissible and advisable; the legislator never intended the precept of making the publications on successive feasts to comprehend this extraordinary instance, where its observance would actually militate against the purpose and efficacy of the banns.[11]

c. *Publication in the Church*

As did the former legislation, so the Code prescribes that the publications be made in the church, the law presuming that the parishioners are assembled there for worship. The parochial church is not specified, and, by comparison with canon 1025—*ecclesiae paroecialis aliusve ecclesiae*—it seems legitimate to infer that the banns can be published in any church in the parish, wherever the pastor, or priest appointed by him to publish the banns, celebrates Mass. The evident intent of the law is, that the banns be published in some sacred edifice, where the parishioners are assembled:[12] in a sacred place, to emphasize their importance, before the assembled congregation, to insure them sufficient publicity.

Canonists have long disputed whether the publications may be made in a public oratory. It seems that they can,[13] provided that the conditions are fulfilled—namely, that the parishioners are present in large numbers, and that a Mass or other divine office is being celebrated by the pastor who has the obligation to make the publications, or by his delegate. For, under the circumstances, the oratory may be regarded as a temporary

---

[10] *Praelectiones Juris Matrimonii*, I, 134.

[11] Wernz-Vidal, *Jus Canonicum*, V, n. 126; De Smet, *Betrothment and Marriage*, I, 30; Chelodi, *Jus Matrimoniale*, n. 26; Noldin, *Summa Theologiae Moralis*, III, n. 552, 2.

[12] Chelodi, *Jus Matrimoniale*, n. 26; Cerato, *Matrimonium*, p. 33.

[13] Wernz-Vidal, *Jus Canonicum*, V, n. 127; Cappello, *De Sacramentis*, III, n. 165, 4; De Smet, *Betrothment and Marriage*, I, 29; Ayrinhac, *Matrimonial Legislation*, p. 57; Augustine, *Commentary*, V, 61.

parish church. Certainly a publication made in the deserted edifice of the parish church would be entirely useless.

When a parish has a chapel of ease (or, as this is sometimes improperly called, a mission station) within its boundaries, and a parishioner, who regularly attends this chapel, wishes to be married, a question arises as to whether the banns may be published there or not. Most canonists now agree that, when the chapel has its own more or less distinct district, and is attended by the people living therein, it will be permissible and sufficient to make the publications there.[14]

A few authors suggest that the pastor may be justified in publishing the banns outside the church building on the occasion of some religious celebration; but they insist that he must have a reasonable cause for this departure from the letter of the law, and should, if time permits, consult the Ordinary. Because of the authority of those who defend it, the view can be admitted, and acted upon, in an emergency at least,—as for example, when the banns were forgotten at Mass, and at the other divine offices in the church, and there is no other opportunity to make the publications. In practice, there will seldom be a religious function which does not either begin or end in the church edifice.[15]

d. *Publication at Mass or Other Frequented Divine Office*

As a general rule, the banns are published at Mass. This need not be a solemn Mass, nor the parochial Mass,[16] but it should be a Mass that is well attended, and celebrated with some solem-

---

[14] Knecht, *Katholisches Eherecht*, p. 172, denies this, as does Augustine, in his *Commentary*, V, 272. On the other side, as proponents of the view, may be numbered: Wernz-Vidal, *Jus Canonicum*, V, n. 127; Vlaming, *Praelectiones Juris Matrimonii*, I, 137; De Smet, *Betrothment and Marriage*, I, 29; Fourneret, *Le Mariage Chrétien*, p. 105; Tanquerey, *Synopsis Theologiae Moralis*, I, n. 884; and Farrugia, *De Matrimonio*, n. 63.

[15] The view is proposed by Prümmer, *Manuale Theologiae Moralis*, III, n. 738; Aertnys-Damen, *Theologia Moralis*, II, n. 678; Tanquerey, *op. cit.*, n. 884; and, under the previous legislation, was supported by St. Alphonsus, *Theologia Moralis*, VI, n. 991, Gasparri, *De Matrimonio*, n. 169, and others.

[16] Cappello, *De Sacramentis*, III, n. 165, 5; Cerato, *Matrimonium*, p. 33.

nity.[17] The general practice in the United States is to publish the banns at the last Mass, which is usually a *Missa cantata* or *solemnis,* and which is as a rule the best attended.

The publications do not have to be made at Mass, however; the pastor can publish the banns at any of the divine offices, provided that there is a sufficiently large gathering of the parishioners present. He can make this substitution on his own authority, and without any special cause.

Just what services are included under the term *divina officia* is not indicated. The Code gives a definition in canon 2256, but restricts its use to that section of the law, and necessarily limits the ambit of the term there to its strictest meaning.[18] In connection with the banns, the term *divina officia* can be regarded as including all acts of public worship for which the people are assembled in the church,—as for instance, Vespers, processions, Exposition of the Blessed Sacrament, the exercises of a mission or retreat, and sermons.[19]

Art. 2. Written Publication

Canon 1025. Potest loci Ordinarius pro suo territorio publicationibus substituere publicam, ad valvas ecclesiae paroecialis aliusve ecclesiae, affixionem nominum contrahentium per spatium saltem octo dierum, ita tamen ut, hoc spatio, duo dies festi de praecepto comprehendantur.

The method of publication outlined in canon 1025 is a concession to modern urban conditions. While written notice of publication was used in certain dioceses as far back as the seven-

[17] In view of conditions as they exist in many large city parishes, where no more than a small portion of the flock is present even at the most crowded Mass, it would be well for the pastor either to publish the banns at all the Sunday Masses, or better, to request the Ordinary to authorize the substitution of the written method of publication. A further discussion of this problem is given in the following articles of this chapter.

[18] Thus, preaching does not come under the prescriptions of canon 2256: Sole, *De Delictis et Poenis,* n. 232.

[19] Cappello, *De Sacramentis,* III, n. 165, 6.

teenth century,[20] it functioned as a subsidiary to, and not as a substitute for oral publication. The first example of this present concession is the privilege accorded the Archbishop of Paris in 1908.[21]

Though this form of publication enjoys many evident advantages over the old practice, individual pastors cannot make the substitution at will, but must apply to the Ordinary.

The action of the Ordinary in this case is not in the nature of a dispensation from the law, nor from the circumstances of the law, but is a simple substitution of another method of publication, dictated by the Ordinary's judgment, and not dependent in any way on the existence of a canonical cause for dispensation. The success of the experiment with this method in Paris, as recounted by Fourneret,[22] would probably attend its introduction into other dioceses. It seems certain that if it were adopted as a partial substitute for oral publication,—that is, if the posting of the written notice were arranged as the equivalent of the second and third oral publication,[23] it would contribute greatly to the effectiveness of the banns, and would relieve the already congested calendar of announcements, common in the larger parishes.[24]

The power of substituting the written publications for the oral is denied to pastors, and reserved to the local Ordinary. Those enjoying this power and title will be more fully desig-

---

[20] Provincial Council of Naples, 1699, t. iii, c. 9, n. 3—*Coll. Lac.*, I, 198. Barbosa noted that it was in use in Spain before the Council of Trent—*Collectanea Doctorum*, p. 574.

[21] S. C. C., 28 Mart. 1908—*A. S.*, XLI [1908], 246. Blat, *Commentarium Textus*, III, i, 520, declares that it obtained as a custom in the United States, and elsewhere; this is difficult to verify. The concession bears a strong resemblance to the French civil law inaugurated in 1907.

[22] Fourneret, *Le Mariage Chrétien*, p. 110.

[23] As in Mechlin: Provincial Council of Mechlin, 1923, n. 208—*Ephemerides Theologicae Lovanienses* I [1924], 559.

[24] The Ordinary would have to consult the Holy See before instituting this partial substitution, because it is not according to the letter of the law. It was introduced in Mechlin by a Provincial Council, all the acts of which were recognized by Rome—(canon 291, § 1), and those contrary to the common law were confirmed *in forma specifica.* Cfr. Van Hove, *De Legibus Eccl.*, p. 350, ftnote 1.

nated in the next chapter, when treating of dispensations from the banns; here, consideration will be limited to the most common situation. The permission is generally to be obtained from the Bishop of the diocese. The Vicar General can also grant the permission, but, since it is a question of introducing so startling an innovation, there is wide room for a conflict between the two authorities, and the possibility that the Vicar General's power would be stayed by canon 369, § 2.

The permission can be given to one or several of the larger parishes in the diocese,[25] or, it can be extended to all parishes, large and small.[26]

The Ordinary cannot prescribe the substitution of written notice for oral announcement in regard to the publications which are to be made in another diocese. His power in this matter is limited by the territorial boundaries of his see—*potest loci Ordinarius pro suo territorio . . . substituere. . . .*

The circumstances of publication under this form differ greatly from those of the traditional method. There is no question here of a triple proclamation, but only of a single publication continued throughout eight days, two of which are feasts of precept. The notice may be posted on any day during the week, but, it must be remembered that, unless one of the six holydays of obligation intervenes, a notice put up on a week day will have to remain on the board for more than eight days, in order to include the two required feasts of precept.

It seems that the day on which the notice is first posted can be counted, as long as the posting took place before the first Mass.[27] In the decree of 1908, the days of publication were described as extending from the first Mass to the last service in the evening. The present law has been changed in part, now demanding a publication continued throughout eight days rather

---

[25] As in Bruges, in 1923:—*Ephemerides Theologicae Lovanienses*, I (1924), 559.

[26] As in Paris, by order of Cardinal Amette, May 6, 1918—Fourneret, *Le Mariage Chrétien*, p. 111; and the Synodal statutes of Paris, 1924, n. 154 (p. 44).

[27] Blat, *Commentarium Textus*, III, i, 520; Fanfani, *De Jure Parochorum*, p. 282; Fourneret, *Le Mariage Chrétien*, p. 111.

than three distinct publications on successive Sundays. However, in the part of the law that has not been changed, it seems admissible to retain the old interpretation, namely, that the requirements of the canon are satisfied, if the notice is posted before the first Mass of the day on which the publication is begun. The law hardly intends to insist that the period of publication begin at midnight in a darkened, deserted church.

Just as the Ordinary may dispense from one or more of the oral publications, so too, it seems, he may reduce the period of time necessary for the written publication.[28]

The place for posting this written publication is at or near the entrance of the church. The church may be the parochial church, or some other church within the limits of the territory subject to the pastor who has the obligation of making the announcement of the particular marriage. What was said on this point, in the preceding section, with regard to the oral publications, applies equally here.

The term *ad valvas,* used in the canon, need not be taken in its literal sense.[29] In fact, a notice placed on the doors of the church might be too easily defaced or tampered with. It is sufficient to post the names—and the other identifying data mentioned above—in a conspicuous place, and preferably in a locked bulletin board. The spot chosen for this must be, not only accessible, but must be so located that the people pass it on their way in and out of church.

After the completion of the period of publication, the prescriptions of canon 1030 must be observed, and the marriage deferred, until three days after the completion of the required period of publication.

* * * * *

In this connection, the writer's attention has been called to a practice obtaining in the Cathedral parish, and certain other parishes of the diocese of Toledo (Ohio, U. S. A.), a practice which merits notice and praise. The banns are first published

---

[28] Fourneret, *Le Mariage Chrétien,* p. 112.

[29] Blat, *Commentarium Textus,* III, i, 520; Fourneret, *Le Mariage Chrétien,* p. 111.

from the pulpit, in the usual way; besides that, however, they are inserted in a printed leaflet of general parochial announcements which is distributed every Sunday at all the Masses. The opinion has already been expressed that publication at every Mass is practically a necessity in the larger parishes in order to insure the banns the proper publicity. But it is precisely in those parishes that the volume of other announcements render this most objectionable. The printed leaflets, on the other hand, will reach all the parishioners, without adding to the burden of the Sunday announcements. This method of publication is an excellent supplement to the oral publications. Whether it can be used as a substitute for them is another question. Needless to say, there is no discussion of the case among authors, and there is no precedent in the law. Publication by leaflet resembles somewhat the method outlined in canon 1025; in fact, it exceeds that method in its publicity value. Many who will not stop to read the posted notices, will read the leaflet, which is handed them; many too, will take it to their homes, and discuss the proposed marriages with members of their families, and their friends. This all adds to the possibility of discovering latent impediments. However, publication by leaflet is not recognized by the law. While the Holy See probably might endorse the practice, if the matter were proposed, still, as far as the writer is aware, it has not as yet been sanctioned, and therefore cannot be admitted as a substitute for either of the two approved modes of publication.

Art. 3. Newspaper Publication

Assuming that the law, as laid down in the Code, has been fully and faithfully observed, and that special efforts have been made to inform as many members of the congregation as possible about a proposed marriage, the publicity thus given is confined to the parishioners actually living in the parish, where the announcements have been made. It fails to reach a wide circle of absent parishioners and former residents, who are well acquainted with the parties, and who may know of the existence of impediments unsuspected by the present parishioners. It must be granted that canon law does not oblige pastors to seek out and inform these absentees, nor was such an obligation ever part of the law. But it cannot be so readily conceded that the divine law does not place some responsibility on those charged with the care of souls, to consult these people, especially when they are numerous, and can be informed about a marriage with a minimum of effort.

The banns were born in an era which had neither the problems of today, nor the agencies for meeting them. The legislation was admirably suited to conditions then existent; and, as a basic law, fashioned to function under various circumstances, in all parts of the world, it is still quite efficient. But, in the face of special difficulties, it becomes expedient to seek relief in supplementary particular legislation.

In every American city, the membership of parishes is constantly shifting; old residents leave a parish and move elsewhere, generally to another parish in the same town or city; seldom do they travel so far as to leave the diocese. It is impossible to conceive of these people immediately severing all ties with their old parish, and forgetting their former neighbors. They retain their interest in them, and that interest could and should be utilized in further safeguarding marriage.

Nearly every diocese in this country has its own official, or quasi-official paper, which could serve as the organ, or as a subsidiary organ for the publication of the banns. Secular authorities in Europe adopted the method of written publication long before the Church; and the civil officials in the United States have long ago taken advantage of the newspapers as channels for matrimonial publication.

Undoubtedly, serious objections can be raised against such a program. The greatest, perhaps, is that it would allow the printer to trespass upon the province of the priest, and, by taking the banns out of the sacred precincts of the church, would lessen the reverence given them. Such a catastrophe is possible—remotely possible, but at its worst, it seems a much lesser evil to risk that, than to endanger the sacredness of marriage itself.

It is true too, that newspaper publication of the banns differs radically from the long established custom of oral proclamation.

The same objection was probably offered when the written method of canon 1025 was first suggested.

Others might object to the financial burden involved in paying for the insertion of the notice in the diocesan paper. But the charge would never be great enough to embarrass even the poorest, and a charge might not even be assessed if the publishers found that the new policy notably increased the paper's circulation—as it probably would.

Against all the drawbacks, alleged or allegeable, what advantages may be urged?

First, the point already stressed, that a publication of the banns in the diocesan paper would appeal to the friends of the parties in all parts of the diocese. And not necessarily the Catholic friends alone; for when the news of the proposed marriage is directly dispensed in the homes of the people, it will be discussed there, and made available to all who will read the notice, Catholic and non-Catholic alike.

Such a policy of publication would, moreover, solve most of the difficulties involved in the faithful and literal observance of canon 1023, §§ 2 and 3.

There would also be less objection to the publishing of mixed marriages in this fashion than there is to it under existing methods, and, if the Ordinary permitted these marriages so to be published, pastors would be greatly assisted in the investigation of the free state of the parties in such cases.

Finally, it would reduce the number of announcements to be made from the pulpit, and the time saved could be devoted to, or added to the period of religious instruction.

Publication by newspaper is not entirely without precedent. Canon 1720 permits a judicial citation to be inserted in a public newspaper. It almost seems an unmerciful procedure, for the Church thus to summon a man to defend his marriage against the accusation of nullity, when it denied him the use of the same means to avert that very disaster. The *Acta Apostolicae Sedis* furnishes another parallel; in times gone by, laws were promulgated by posting them on the church doors, just as the banns are sometimes published today; now the legislator takes advantage of the improvements of science for the better and speedier promulgation of his laws.

Even St. Alphonsus can be construed as condoning this method of publication,[30] for he proposed the view of Bossius and others, which maintained that, when plague or other emergency prevented the convening of the parishioners, the town crier could be permitted to publish the banns. The town crier has been supplanted, as a news agency, by the press, and the emergency has been translated into an ever present necessity.

The plea here advanced for newspaper publication is not meant to advocate the abolition of the oral announcement, nor is it particularly intended to apply to rural parishes. The need it seeks to have filled exists chiefly in the crowded city areas, where the tenure of residence is especially unstable. Therefore the change could be limited to the urban parishes. If the Holy See would permit it, the number of oral publications necessary could be curtailed in view of the publicity afforded by the printed notice. By reducing the number of oral proclamations, the burden of parochial announcements would be greatly reduced, and by the printed notice, a much more numerous audience would be secured.

As a supplementary method of publication, it seems that any Ordinary may introduce it into his diocese, but, be it remembered, the number and circumstances of the publications as outlined in the Code would still be of obligation. Only the Holy See is competent to permit the substitution, or partial substitution of newspaper publication for the methods now allowed.

---

[30] *Theologia Moralis*, VI, n. 991.

CHAPTER IX

EXCEPTIONS TO THE OBLIGATION OF PUBLICATION

The principle enunciated in canon 1022, that the pastor is to announce proposed marriages, suffers certain exception, sometimes by the express command of the law, at other times by the permission of the law, of custom, or of necessity.

ART. 1. MIXED MARRIAGES

Canon 1026. Publicationes ne fiant pro matrimoniis quae contrahuntur cum dispensatione ab impedimento disparitatis cultus aut mixtae religionis, nisi loci Ordinarius pro sua prudentia, remoto scandalo, eas permittere opportunum duxerit, dummodo apostolica dispensatio praecesserit et mentio omittatur religionis partis non catholicae.

First and above all, it is forbidden to publish the banns by oral announcement, when one of the parties is a non-Catholic. It likewise seems almost certain that publication by the written method is prohibited. Canon 1026, it is true, merely forbids the *publicationes*, which in the preceding canon were clearly distinguished from *publica affixio.* But, since the term *publicationes* is used in canons 1029 and 1030 in a sense which obviously includes both oral and written announcement, the conclusion is quite certain that the *publicationes* in canon 1026 is to be taken to mean both species of announcements.

The prohibition of the banns extends to all mixed marriages, that is, all marriages for which there is necessary a dispensation from the impediments of disparity of worship or mixed religion. The banns are not forbidden, but are of strict obligation for marriages that are celebrated after the use of the Pauline Privilege.[1] The same is true with regard to a marriage to be con-

[1] Authors have not discussed this point, but it follows that, since the law has made no exception for such marriages, the banns must be published, or a dispensation from the obligation obtained.

tracted with one who will be received into the Church only on the eve of the wedding. Before the Code, it was maintained by some,[2] that the banns could not be published in such a case until that party had actually been converted. Under the present law, there is not only no prohibition, but, on the contrary, a strict obligation to make the announcements of a marriage between a Catholic, and one who will be a Catholic on the day of the wedding, even though he or she is only a catechumen at the time of the publications.[3]

Another consequence of the very definite restriction placed on the prohibition of the banns by the Code is, that marriages between the faithful and members of condemned societies, or others mentioned in canons 1065 and 1066, however detestable, must be published, unless the Ordinary dispenses with the banns in view of the danger of scandal.

The prohibition of publication in cases of mixed marriage is not absolute, but subject to the discretion of the local Ordinary,[4] who can permit the announcements to be made, once the dispensation from the impediment has been granted, provided that the danger of scandal to the faithful is removed,[5] and the pastors instructed to refrain from mentioning the difference of religion. In countries predominantly non-Catholic, and especially where divorce is rampant, Ordinaries may very well find it opportune to permit the publication of the banns at all mixed marriages. This is particularly true of the United States. Without the banns, there is little or no means of ascertaining the free state of the non-Catholic party. The pastor's investigation is, as a rule, crippled by his lack of acquaintance with that party, and the State offers little cooperation, since it grants a license,

---

[2] *A. E. R.*, LIII [1915], 230; LVIII [1918], 433.

[3] Schenk, *Mixed Religion and Disparity of Cult*, p. 283; *A. E. R.*, LXXIX [1928], 648; Augustine, *Rights and Duties of Ordinaries*, p. 289, denies the obligation of making the publications, but without advancing sufficient reason for his view.

[4] If the parties live in different dioceses, the permission obtained from one Bishop will be effective only in his diocese.

[5] This can be very easily done by explaining to the people the motives impelling the Bishop to adopt such a course.

usually without any attempt to verify the applicant's declaration of freedom.

Art. 2. Marriages of Conscience

Canon 1104. Nonnisi ex gravissima et urgentissima causa et ab ipso loci Ordinario, excluso Vicario Generali sine speciali mandato, permitti potest ut *matrimonium conscientiae* ineatur, idest matrimonium celebretur omissis denuntiationibus et secreto, ad normam canonum qui sequuntur.

Of the exception granted in canon 1104, little need be said. When circumstances are such that the marriage must be celebrated secretly before the pastor and two witnesses, and the Ordinary sees fit to grant that permission, it follows logically and necessarily that a public announcement of the proposed marriage is entirely out of place.

Art. 3. Cases of Necessity

Situations occur not infrequently when a couple, face to face with some emergency, request the celebration of their marriage immediately, even though none of the customary publications has been made. If the necessity is caused by the danger of death of one or both of the parties, there is no doubt that the obligation to publish the banns ceases, because the law itself provides for that.[6]. Some canonists restrict their concept of emergency to this case.[7]

But, there are other instances in which, due to some other reason—for example, when the man is suddenly and unexpectedly called upon to undertake a protracted journey, and his spouse is already pregnant—marriage cannot be postponed until the banns have been duly published, or even dispensed, without exposing the parties to the danger of grave loss. The pastor must undoubtedly conduct his personal investigation. It will

---

[6] Canon 1019, § 2.

[7] Tanquerey, *Synopsis Theologiae Moralis,* I, n. 889. Vermeersch-Creusen, *Epitome,* II, n. 291, holds that the emergency which would justify the total omission of the banns (without dispensation) is only very rarely verified outside of the danger of death.

be assumed for present purposes that at the conclusion of that examination he is assured that the parties are free to marry. He is then faced with the problem of the banns. If it is possible to delay the marriage ceremony long enough to make one or two of the publications, or to seek a dispensation, total or partial according to the circumstances, from one who has the faculty of granting it, he is obliged to that degree of compliance with the law. If this is not possible, but he is certain that the parties are free, and is equally certain that a further postponement of the marriage will entail a grave loss, spiritual or temporal, for the couple, even though he has been unable to make any of the publications, the pastor may declare that the obligation of the banns no longer urges in the case.[8] For when these two conditions are simultaneously present, compliance with the law is not only useless, but also positively harmful, and the legislator cannot be regarded as insisting upon its observance.[9]

Although strictly speaking a dispensation is not necessary when an emergency such as has been described exists, still in practice the Ordinary should be consulted, if time permits. He may either go through the form of granting a dispensation, or may simply declare that the law has ceased to bind in the case. The pastor should take the responsibility of issuing the declaration only as a last resort; the Ordinary is the proper one to pass judgment on all such questions.

Before the Code, authors counseled the pastor to inform his Ordinary after the ceremony that he had omitted the publications owing to the emergency. They had very good reason for insisting on that course of action, because under the old law the Bishop could order the publication of the banns after the marriage ceremony, and could forbid the consummation of the marriage until the publications had been completed. He cannot do this any longer.[10] In consequence, the pastor is no longer

---

[8] Cappello, *De Sacramentis*, III, n. 162, 3; Wernz-Vidal, *Jus Canonicum*, V, n. 123; Aertnys-Damen, *Theologia Moralis*, II, n. 683.

[9] Van Hove, *De Legibus Ecclesiasticis*, n. 291.

[10] Canon 1022. The obligation to make the publications exists only before the marriage—*inter quosnam matrimonium sit contrahendum.* The consummation of the marriage cannot be forbidden, for canon 1111 recognizes the rights of the parties in that matter *ab ipso matrimonii initio.*

obliged by the common law to report to the Ordinary after assisting at such a marriage.[11]

Art. 4. Princely Marriages

The marriages of princes have generally been regarded as exempt from the law of the banns, and the reason behind the exemption is that the marriages of royalty and the higher nobility do not need the artificially stimulated publicity of the banns; their matrimonial plans are matter of public knowledge.

The nature or basis of the exemption may be defined as a privilege acquired by custom.[12] As such it has survived the Code, according to the prescriptions of canon 4; for although there is no evidence in available sources to show that the privilege was ever expressly conceded by the Holy See, nevertheless centenary possession induces the presumption that such a concession was made.[13]

The exact extent of the exemption was never very clearly established, but it certainly includes those persons of princely rank described in canon 1557, § 1, 1°. The privilege was not accorded princes in view of their exalted political and social position, but merely because of the accidental acquaintance with their lives and doings which the public enjoys. Hence, a parity cannot be established between the rulers of royal lineage in canon 1557, and those other actual and proximate executives of humbler origin, who guide the destiny of democracies.

Art. 5. Dispensation

Canon 1028, § 1. Loci Ordinarius proprius pro suo prudenti judicio potest ex legitima causa a publica-

---

[11] Cappello, *De Sacramentis,* III, n. 168.

[12] Canon 63, § 1. Several authors are satisfied with tracing it to custom—thus, Rossi, *De Matrimonii Celebratione,* n. 14; Tanquerey, *Synopsis Theologiae Moralis,* I, n. 881; Cappello, *De Sacramentis,* III, n. 162; and others. But it must be remembered that, if custom is its only foundation, it is a custom that is contrary to the law, and *per se* should be suppressed. (Canon 5).

[13] Canon 63, § 2. Ojetti, *Commentarium in Codicem,* I, 284; Maroto, *Institutiones Juris Canonici,* I, 353.

tionibus etiam in aliena dioecesi faciendis dispensare.

Canon 1028, § 2. Si plures sint Ordinarii proprii, ille jus habet dispensandi, in cujus dioecesi matrimonium celebratur; quod si matrimonium extra proprias ineatur dioeceses, quilibet Ordinarius proprius dispensare potest.

Dispensation is the most frequently encountered source of exemption from the obligation of the banns.

a. *The Author of the Dispensation*

In keeping with the former discipline, local Ordinaries are empowered to dispense from the banns. The Code very clearly defines the extension of the term "local Ordinary." Besides the Roman Pontiff, the following are classed under this category: residential Bishops, Abbots and Prelates *Nullius,* and the Vicars General of all three; Administrators, Vicars, and Prefects Apostolic;[14] and finally, those who by law or approved constitutions succeed the aforementioned during a vacancy or other impediment of office. Thus, the Chapter of the Cathedral (canon 431), Abbacy or Prelature (canon 324), before the election of a Vicar Capitular; the Vicar Capitular (canon 435); and in mission countries, the Pro-Vicar and Pro-Prefect Apostolic (canon 309, § 2). In the dioceses of the United States, the functions of the Chapter and the Vicar Capitular are fulfilled, respectively, by the Diocesan Consultors and the Administrator of the vacant diocese.[15] All these, since they enjoy ordinary power to dispense from the banns, may, by virtue of canon 199, § 1, delegate others to do the same.

Legates of the Holy See do not enjoy the faculty of dispensing

[14] Vicars and Prefects Apostolic are not allowed to appoint Vicars General; they may however appoint Vicars Delegate, who enjoy all the powers of jurisdiction which the Vicar or Prefect Apostolic has, excepting those which the Vicar or Prefect reserves to himself, or which by law require a special mandate. (S. C. de Prop. Fide, litt. 8 Dec. 1919,—*A. A. S.*, XII [1920], 120. Cfr. *Periodica de Re Can.*, IX [1921], (24).

[15] III Plenary Council of Baltimore, 1884, t. ii, c. 2, n. 18,—*Acta et Decreta Conc. Plen. Balt. III*, p. 14. Canon 427.

from the banns. Neither do Vicars Forane, nor pastors, nor any of the inferior clerics possess this power, unless it has been granted to them by the Ordinary of one of the parties.

Vlaming[16] holds that pastors and the other priests mentioned in canons 1044 and 1098, § 2 have the faculty of dispensing from the banns when one or both of the parties is in danger of death. It is difficult to concede this, since the Code itself in canon 1019, § 2 expressly states that the publications are not of obligation under the circumstances, if they cannot be made.

Canon 1045, § 3 does not concede to pastors the power of dispensing from the banns. The case contemplated in that canon is one in which an impediment is unexpectedly discovered, and under circumstances which preclude the possibility of getting a dispensation from the impediment through the regular channels. But, if the banns have been omitted in the case, through forgetfulness or other cause, and the omission is discovered too late to make the publications or to seek a dispensation from them, it being impossible to postpone the marriage without grave inconvenience to the parties, the case of necessity, treated above, may be verified, but certainly not the situation considered in canon 1045, § 3.

Canon 1028 stresses the limitation placed on the Ordinary's power in canons 201, § 1, by using the expression *loci Ordinarius proprius.* Whatever may be said on the general question of dispensation,[17] the Code has settled the matter with regard to the banns, since it expressly requires that the dispensation come from one's proper Ordinary. The argument might be advanced that because the Ordinary is given the faculties to dispense

---

[16] *Praelectiones Juris Matrimonii,* I, 143.

[17] A few authors maintain that a Bishop can dispense *peregrini* in his diocese—thus Maroto, *Institutiones,* I, n. 305; Ferreres, *Theologia Moralis,* I, n. 184. The preferable opinion is that the Bishop may dispense only his subjects, that is, those who have a domicile or quasi-domicile in the diocese, and *vagi* actually residing within the territory—with the exception of those cases in which express provision is made for the dispensing of *peregrini,* as in canons 1043, 1045, 1245, 1313, 1320, and the quinquennial faculties. This view is upheld by Chelodi, *Jus de Personis,* n. 153; Ojetti, *Commentarium in Codicem,* I, 329; and Kinane, in the *I. E. R.,* XXXV [1930], 295.

peregrini from matrimonial impediments, *a fortiori* he should have the power to dispense them from the banns. In reality there is no comparison between the two dispensations. The impediment in the one case, is known to exist, and all that is necessary on the Bishop's part is that he be assured of the presence of a just cause for relaxing the law. His judgment is a judgment on an existent and known fact, and is independent of any acquaintance with the status of the parties. On the other hand, a dispensation from the banns entails more than a judgment on the cause necessary for the granting of the dispensation. In giving the dispensation from the publications, the Ordinary eliminates a very important part of the prenuptial investigation, and in effect declares that it is safe to omit it. He will ordinarily rely on the recommendation of the pastor who submits the request for the dispensation. If that is one of the priests of his own diocese, where the parties in question are only visitors, that priest, in the ordinary case, will not have any great assurance of the freedom of the parties; if, on the other hand, that priest is in the diocese where the parties have their domiciles, it will be difficult to understand why he does not make application to his own Bishop, who is also the proper Ordinary of the parties.

A still more serious objection to the dispensing of *peregrini* from the banns arises independently of this matter of acquaintance with the parties.

As has been pointed out before, the obligation of the banns rests only indirectly and in a secondary way on the parties; the pastor is the one who is bound primarily and directly. Canon 1028, § 1 directs that the proper Ordinary grant the dispensation—that is, the proper Ordinary of both the pastor and the parties, for the parties are always subject to the same Ordinary as their proper pastor is. The Code reserves the power to dispense to that Ordinary, to whom the pastor who has the obligation to publish the banns is subject; and, if there are several pastors in different dioceses bound to make the publications in a given case, *per se* it would seem that each Ordinary had to dispense each pastor. But the legislator in the Code, profiting by the controversies existent under the old law, has empowered any one of these several Bishops to dispense all the pastors concerned, even in the other dioceses—reserving the *right* to dispense, in case the marriage is to take place in the diocese of one of these proper Ordinaries, to that Ordinary. Applying these principles to the present problem, namely, the power of a Bishop to dispense from the banns in the case of two *peregrini* in his diocese: if the pastor who requests the dispensation is the pastor of the parish where the parties are staying as *peregrini*, he is asking to be dispensed from an obligation to which he is in no way subject, for the Code places the obligation of publishing the banns only on the proper pastors of the parties; if, on the other hand, the pastor of the parish in which the parties have their domicile or quasi-domicile, makes the request for the dispensation to the Ordinary of the diocese where the parties are staying as *peregrini*, he is asking to be freed from an obligation by a Bishop to whom he is in no way subject.

Therefore there seems to be no basis for the assertion that a Bishop may dispense from the banns for the marriage of *peregrini* in his diocese; to grant the dispensation, he would need delegation from one of the proper Ordinaries.

The Code has given these proper Ordinaries the power to dispense, and ordained that their dispensations are effective not only in their own dioceses, but in every place where there is an obligation to make the publications.[18]

Canon 1028, § 2, however, places a restriction on the power of Ordinaries, by reserving the right of dispensing to that one of the proper Ordinaries in whose diocese the marriage is to take place. If the marriage is scheduled to be celebrated in a diocese not proper to either of the parties, the powers of both their proper Ordinaries remain intact, and either can grant the favor.

The limitation introduced in this section of the canon aims at reducing the possibility of a conflict of jurisdiction. Unfortunately, it leaves one point rather vague, for it fails to indicate with certainty whether the restriction affects the validity or

[18] Canon 1028, § 1 in conjunction with 201, § 3. The Ordinary may, if he chooses, limit the dispensation to the pastors of his own diocese.

merely the liceity of acts placed in violation of it. The question hinges on the interpretation of the phrase *ille jus habet dispensandi,* taken in conjunction with the *dispensare potest* which follows it. Canonists have given the difficulty little attention, and the few who have discussed it, differ in their opinions.

Kinane[19] maintains that when the marriage is to be contracted in the diocese of one of the proper Ordinaries, only he can validly dispense. The argument he advances is this: . . . "If it be remembered that the obligation of having the banns proclaimed arises from the general law, and that therefore the power to dispense from it is not innate in the office of local Ordinary, but is something superadded to it by law; and in the circumstances under consideration only the Ordinary of the place in which the marriage takes place is declared to have the power of dispensing."

Cappello[20], the only other author who goes into the matter, is of the opinion that the restriction in this canon does not interfere with the validity of a dispensation given in contravention of it.

Dr. Kinane seems to view the situation from the wrong angle. The second section of canon 1028 does not give the Ordinary any power; it does not superadd, but actually restricts the general power given him in the preceding section of the canon. The point at issue is not to determine how much power is here given the Ordinary, but how much is taken away.

A restriction like this, militating as it does against ordinary power, must be given a strict interpretation.[21] The Bishop is granted the ordinary power to dispense with the banns for marriages of his own subjects—even though absent from the diocese[22], and he retains his right, until, and only in so far as it is restricted, and the restriction proved. It is true that canon 1028, § 2 limits the use of the dispensing faculty, but it does not indicate that its prescriptions affect the validity of acts placed

[19] *I. E. R.,* XXXV [1930], 646; and perhaps Chelodi, *Jus Matrimoniale,* n. 28—though his statement is somewhat ambiguous.

[20] *De Sacramentis,* III, n. 169.

[21] Canon 200, § 1.

[22] Canon 201, § 3.

in violation of its mandates. Yet, unless a law expressly or equivalently states that its restrictions affect the validity of the acts forbidden or commanded, no argument for the invalidity of those acts can be established.[23]

The only basis allegeable for maintaining the invalidity of a dispensation in the case under consideration, would be had in the phrase *ille jus habet*, by itself, or taken in conjunction with the words *dispensare potest*, which follow it.

Taken alone, the term *ille jus habet* can furnish no argument, for it would follow that all such reservations throughout the Code involved validity—thus, no one but the proper pastor could validly administer Baptism,[24] and in the celebration of marriage, the old Tridentine regulations, contained in the decree "*Tametsi,*" would have to be revived.

Even considering the two terms in conjunction, the arguments fails to prove that a dispensation would be invalidly granted against the norms laid down in this section of canon 1028. To take the two expressions together would be, in effect, to read the words *dispensare non potest* into the first clause of the section, and to predicate them of all the proper Ordinaries, except the one in whose diocese the marriage is to take place. Such a construction could hardly be adjudged as in accordance with the rules of logic, and certainly would differ from the evident meaning of the combinations of the same or similar terms as used elsewhere in the Code.[25]

The pre-Code interpretation sheds little light on the problem. Even among authors who regarded the dispensation of one Bishop as sufficient, few of them did more than recommend the reserving of the right of dispensing to the Bishop of the place where the marriage was to take place.[26]

All things being considered, then, it seems at least quite probable, that canon 1028, § 2 merely denies the other proper Ordinaries the licit exercise of their faculty of dispensing from the banns, when the marriage is to take place in the diocese of one proper Ordinary.

[23] Canon 11.

[24] Canon 738, § 1.

[25] Thus, canons 848, §§ 1 and 2; 738, § 2; 938, § 2.

[26] Wernz, *Jus Decretalium*, IV, 190; Gasparri, *De Matrimonio*, n. 183.

If the marriage is to be contracted in the territory of a Prelate to whom neither party is subject, any proper Ordinary of either party may validly and lawfully dispense from obligation of the banns, not only the pastors of his own diocese who would have had to make the publications, but, by virtue of the power given him by the Code, he can dispense all other pastors upon whom the obligation is incumbent.

b. *The Dispensation Itself*

A dispensation can be either total or partial—that is, it can remove the obligation of making any publication in any parish, or it can be so limited as to release a certain pastor from making any publication, or to release one or all pastors from making one or two publications. Ordinaries generally grant dispensations in such a way as to affect all pastors upon whom rests the duty of publishing a particular marriage; on the other hand, they usually limit the dispensations in regard to the number of publications waived.

Dispensations may even be limited to a relaxation of the solemnity of the publications. That is to say, the pastor may be permitted to make the publication on a feast of rank lesser than those indicated in canon 1024. Although the Code does not explicitly mention this procedure, it is generally recognized by authors, and is based on the proposition that one who can do the greater thing can also do a lesser thing contained therein.[27] Bishops can no longer order the publication of the banns deferred until after the marriage ceremony.[28]

c. *The Form and Duration of the Dispensation*

With regard to the form of the dispensation itself, the law prescribes nothing other than that it be given in writing.[29] In some diocese, special blanks are prepared both for the applica-

[27] R. 35, R. J., in VI: "Plus semper in se continet, quod est minus." And also the corollary, R. 53, R. J., in VI: "Cui licet, quod est plus, licet utique, quod est minus."

[28] Canon 1022: "inter quosnam matrimonium sit contrahendum."

[29] Canon 56. This merely affects the liceity of the concession.

tion for, and the concession of the dispensation. This relieves the pastor and Curia of much unnecessary work, and secures uniformity in the records.

While no authority can be adduced by the writer for the following statement, still it seems logical to maintain that the petition for this dispensation should be made out in the name of the pastor, rather than in the names of the parties, because it is upon the pastor that the obligation of publishing the banns rests primarily and directly. The names of the parties would have to be inserted in the petition, but only for the purpose of identifying the case.

No fee can be demanded for this dispensation,[30] but some remuneration may be asked—unless the petitioners are poor—to cover the expenses of chancery. Some authors regard it as lawful for the Ordinary to request in addition, a donation for pious causes.[31] This view cannot be condemned, but if the Ordinary chooses to follow it, he must bear in mind that his request cannot be made after the manner of a precept, and that any donation made by the parties must be entirely voluntary.[32]

The law is silent with regard to the length of time during which the dispensation remains in force. In view of the prescriptions of canon 1030, § 2, which demand the repetition of the publications after six months, it seems that, unless the Ordinary declares otherwise, the dispensation from the banns lapses after six months, computed from the date of its issue. If the parties then wished to be married without having the banns proclaimed, another dispensation would be necessary.

d. *The Causes for Granting Dispensations*

A local Ordinary cannot validly dispense from the banns without a legitimate cause, since the law is not his own, but his Superior's. Authors, following the injunctions of Benedict

---

[30] Canon 1056. Also, S. C. de Prop. Fide, 12 Feb. 1821—*Coll. P. F.*, n. 755; III Plen. Council of Baltimore, t. iv, n. 134.

[31] Noldin, *Summa Theologiae Moralis*, III, n. 618; *A. E. R.*, III [1890], 16; LII [1915], 348.

[32] Vromant, *De Bonis Ecclesiae Temporalibus*, n. 110.

XIV,[33] have insisted on the need of a just cause for dispensing from one publication, and a proportionately greater reason for a more extensive dispensation. Though it would be impractical, and even impossible, to grade these causes categorically, the general distinction serves as an index to the mind of the legislator. The Code did not introduce any relaxation regarding these dispensations; the term *ex legitima causa* in canon 1028, § 1, is not to be taken as synonymous with *causa levis,* but is to be interpreted in the light of pre-Code teaching.

Canonists suggest a number of reasons which would justify a Bishop in dispensing from the banns: thus, the fear of malicious interference with the celebration of the marriage; the danger of scandal or infamy involved in delaying the marriage; the danger of incontinence or other loss to the parties; the approach of the *tempus clausum*; the possibility that the parties would be exposed to ridicule if the banns were published, as for example, when their ages or social positions are greatly disparate.[34] None of these lists is proposed as taxative. As under the previous legislation, so now, any cause may be alleged, which the Ordinary judges to be sufficient. He may of course insist that one of the recognized canonical causes[35] be verified before he grants a dispensation. This is fully within his power, and in some dioceses has been determined by statute.[36]

Canonists go so far as to recognize the liceity of the Ordinary's action in granting a dispensation merely upon the request of the parties, when he is certain that there is no impediment

---

[33] Benedictus XIV, ep. encycl., "*Etsi minime,*" 7 Feb. 1742, n. 10; ep. encycl., "*Nimiam licentiam,*" 18 Maii 1743, n. 14—*Fontes,* nn. 324 and 337. Cfr. Gasparri, *De Matr.,* n. 187; D'Annibale, *Summula Theologiae Moralis,* III, n. 453, 7; and others.

[34] Cfr. Cappello, *De Sacramentis,* III, n. 168; Vermeersch-Creusen, *Epitome,* II, n. 291; De Smet, *Betrothment and Marriage,* I, 30; and authors generally. The most complete list is given by Ferraris, *Prompta Bibliotheca,* art. "Matrimonium," IV, n. 22, wherein he lists fifteen causes.

[35] Cfr. S. C. de Prop. Fide, instr., 8 May, 1877—*Coll. P. F.,* # 1470; Dataria Apostolica, formula pro matrimonialibus dispensationibus, 1901—*A. S.,* XXXIV [1901-02], 34,—in so far as these are applicable to the banns.

[36] Thus, in Passau—*A. k. KR.,* LII [1909], 739; and according to De Smet, *Betrothment and Marriage,* I, 34, in the diocese of Bruges, 1910.

present.[37] The basis for the dispensation in this case is that the principal purpose of the law has ceased, and for that reason the Ordinary is justified in granting the dispensation, even from all publications, without seeking further canonical cause. Lacking moral certainty of the freedom of the parties, even though there is no positive doubt about that freedom, the Ordinary cannot grant a dispensation, unless some legitimate cause for dispensation is verified. Finally, if the Ordinary has reason to suspect the presence of an impediment to the marriage, he may not grant a dispensation from the banns, at least not from all publications, until the suspicion is removed.[38]

Although a Bishop may take advantage of the above mentioned opinion and grant a dispensation merely on the ground of his certainty that the purpose of the law has ceased, the procedure is not commendable. If done rarely, it gives every appearance of favoritism. If done generally, it paves the way for serious abuse, since the Bishop is generally dependent on the individual pastors for his assurance, whose advice may not always be prudent and well founded in fact.

Those endowed with power to dispense from the banns should exercise their prerogative with great hesitancy and caution. At times the spiritual or temporal good of the parties would be notably injured by a denial of a dispensation; in those instances the Ordinary is bound in conscience to grant it, unless there is present a grave doubt about the freedom of the parties, which cannot be removed without the publication of the banns. In other cases, the Ordinary may grant or deny the favor, as he sees fit, even though the cause alleged is sufficient to justify him in dispensing. It is precisely in his evaluation of the various causes presented that he employs the prudence which the legislator demands of those who enjoy this important faculty of dispensing.

---

[37] Cappello, *De Sacramentis*, III, n. 168, 3; Tanquerey, *Synopsis Theologiae Moralis*, I, n. 890; De Smet, *Betrothment and Marriage*, I, 35; and, under the old law, St. Alphonsus, *Theologia Moralis*, VI, n. 1006; and others.

[38] Rossi, *De Matrimonii Celebratione*, n. 17; Gasparri, *De Matrimonio*, n. 186.

CHAPTER X

THE OBLIGATION OF REVEALING IMPEDIMENTS

Canon 1027. Omnes fideles tenentur impedimenta, si qua norint, parocho aut loci Ordinario, ante materimonii celebrationem, revelare.

Unless the faithful were obliged to manifest to the pastor the impediments to a marriage of which they have knowledge, the banns would be useless, and the canons dealing with them superfluous.

The obligation declared in canon 1027 is not merely an ecclesiastical precept; the Code incorporates and declares the divine law. The seeming limitation contained in the canon, when it decrees that all the faithful are bound to reveal impediments, does not at all exclude others from this duty. The ecclesiastical obligation can be placed only on baptized persons, whereas the divine law extends to all. All, therefore, who have knowledge of the existence of an impediment, and who are not privileged, are bound, out of charity to the parties, and out of respect to the sacrament, to make that impediment known to the proper authorities. The obligation is in itself undoubtedly grave, since the object of the law is most serious: the welfare of religion, of the commonweal, of the parties, and of their offspring is involved.[1] There is a duty, therefore, and a serious one, to make known any impediment or other obstacle to marriage, whether the impediment is impedient or diriment, whether certain or probable.[2]

---

[1] Wernz-Vidal, *Jus Canonicum*, V, n. 131; Cappello, *De Sacramentis*, III, n. 171; Tanquerey, *Synopsis Theologiae Moralis*, I, n. 891; Noldin, *Summa Theologiae Moralis*, III, n. 554; De Smet, *Betrothment and Marriage*, I, 36. The obligation can be enforced, on baptized persons, with canonical penalties.

[2] De Smet, *Betrothment and Marriage*, I, 36; Noldin, *Summa Theologiae Moralis*, III, n. 554; Cappello, *De Sacramentis*, III, n. 171; Vlaming, *Praelectiones Juris Matr.*, n. 166.

The view cannot be maintained that there is no obligation to report an impediment whose existence cannot be juridically proved. This old opinion was based on a misapplication of the rules of evidence. There is no question here of declaring the nullity of a marriage already contracted, but of preventing an unlawful union. Hence, anyone who knows of an impediment is bound to make it known; the occult nature of the impediment offers no excuse. This obligation extends to the relatives of the parties and the parties themselves—in fact, it rests on them above all.

Even though one is not certain that the impediment exists, it seems that there is an obligation to make known one's suspicion, provided it is well founded.[3] Information based on a vague and uncertain rumor, or on the mere prating of a gossip need not be relayed to the pastor, unless there is the possibility of testing the truth of the rumor by a more diligent investigation.

Though the Code expressly states that the report should be made before the celebration of the marriage, that determination must not be interpreted as ending the obligation, but as urging it. Both the divine and ecclesiastical law impose this duty before the marriage, but the mandates of both retain their force after the marriage, as long as the impediment exists. When the report is made previously to the celebration of the marriage, the certain testimony of one reliable person based upon personal knowledge, (and in certain circumstances, even other sources of information are admissible) is sufficient to prevent the wedding, or postpone it until a dispensation has been obtained;[4] even when the report is based on merely probable knowledge it will lead the pastor to make a more searching investigation, and to seek a dispensation for the parties, if

[3] Tanquerey, *Synopsis Theologiae Moralis*, I, 892, and others state that an obligation is present only when one has certain knowledge of the impediment. But in their explanations, they seem to extend the term "certain" to all well founded information.

[4] C. 22, X, *de testibus et attest.*, II, 20; c. 12, X, *de sponsalibus et matrim.*, IV, I; S. C. C., *in causa Varmien.*, 14 Jun. 1874—*A. S.*, VIII, 1874, 211; Mascardus, *De Probationibus*, con. 1033, n. 2; Schmalzgrueber, *Jus Eccl.*, IX, 365; Sanchez, *De Matr.*, I, d. 71, nn. 1-5; St. Alphonsus, *Theologia Moralis*, VI, nn. 996-7; Ballerini-Palmieri, *Opus Theol. Morale*, VI, 908; Cerato, *Matrimonium*, p. 35.

necessary. Once the marriage has been contracted, one reporting the existence of an impediment is always open to the suspicion of malice,[5] provided of course that the person was in a position to make the report at the proper time. Furthermore, the principle laid down in canon 1014 has by that time become operative, and accusations must meet the requirements of judicial proof in order to establish the nullity of a marriage—if the impediment proves to be indispensable, and there is only the unsupported testimony of one person to prove its existence, the parties will find themselves in a most unfortunate position.

Canon 1027 further directs that the denunciation of the impediment be made to the pastor or Ordinary. It passes over in silence, but it does not exclude the revealing of the impediment to the parties themselves. Generally it will be sufficient to make it known to them; and certainly when the impediment is defamatory, charity makes it imperative for the informant to give the one laboring under the impediment an opportunity to preserve his reputation, unless there is not sufficient time in which to reach that person before the marriage, or the informant is certain that the party will disregard his admonition.

When the assistant is conducting the prenuptial investigation in the pastor's place, the reporting of the impediment is to be made to him.

Those Excused from the Obligation of Reporting Impediments: It has been said that anyone who knows of the existence of an impediment, is bound to make it known. The obligation suffers some exceptions, similar to those established with regard to jurdical testimony, in canons 1755, § 2, 1° and 2°, and 1757, § 3, 2°.[6] The question of exemption here is primarily a moral question, and therefore, only a brief summary will be given.

First, knowledge gained through confessional sources is absolutely excluded. This applies not only to the confessor himself, but to all others, who may have accidentally overheard the confession. The exemption is admitted by all authors.[7]

---

[5] C. 6, X, *qui matrimonium accusare possunt*, IV, 17.

[6] Leitner, *Katholisches Eherecht*, p. 262.

[7] De Smet, *Betrothment and Marriage*, I, 39, would allow the confessor to use the knowledge acquired in the confessional to obtain a dispensation from an occult impediment, when he finds it inexpedient to advise the penitent of the existence of the impediment.

Theologians are also practically unanimous[8] in exempting the knowledge gained by professional men and women, in the exercise of their offices as public advisers and counselors—thus priests, doctors, nurses, lawyers. The interests of the community demand that such information be ever kept inviolate, lest public confidence be shaken. However, authors warn these people that they have a duty to try, as far as prudently possible, to dissuade their clients, who labor under an impediment, from marrying without obtaining a dispensation.

The obligation of private individuals to maintain natural and promised secrets yields, all theologians agree, to the duty of preventing unlawful marriages. Theological opinion is also predominantly in favor of denying any special privilege to committed secrets; in fact, Wernz-Vidal[9] is about the only prominent author, who stands for the opposite, and the view can hardly be called probable.

On the score of secrecy, therefore, the only exceptions to the obligation of revealing are the exemptions of confessional knowledge, and of that gained in the exercise of professional duties.

Danger of loss or injury to the informant also exerts some excusing influence. When a loss or injury proportioned to the consequences of his silence threatens the one reporting the impediment, or his close relatives, as a result of his revelations, he is certainly excused from the duty.[10] The same is true if the public would suffer, in the way of scandal, or other loss. Some theologians maintain that, if a grave loss would befall a third party—not the contracting parties themselves, though, unless the loss is the very gravest—that danger would also suffice to excuse one from making the denunciation.[11]

Authors also assert that it is permissible to omit the report,

---

[8] Sanchez, *De Matrimonio,* III, d. 13, n. 5; Schmalzgrueber, *Jus Eccl. Univ.,* IV, iii, n. 54, and a few others held the opposite.

[9] Wernz-Vidal, *Jus Canonicum,* V, n. 131.

[10] De Smet, *Betrothment and Marriage,* I, 38; Vermeersch-Creusen, *Theologia Moralis,* III, n. 746; Cappello, *De Sacramentis,* III, n. 173, 4; and authors generally.

[11] Fanfani, *De Jure Parochorum,* n. 282; Vermeersch-Creusen, *Epitome,* III, n. 292; Tanquerey, *Synopsis Theologiae Moralis,* I, n. 892; Cappello, *De Sacramentis,* III, n. 173, 4.

when it is obviously useless to make it.[12] This can happen, for instance, when one is certain that the pastor is fully aware of the existence of the impediment, or when one knows that a dispensation has been obtained.

* * * * *

As a natural consequence of this obligation which is put upon the faithful, another is placed upon the priests, and that is, to instruct the people in the Church's laws on marriage: the impediments, the various sources of defect in matrimonial consent, and the grave obligation incumbent upon them of revealing any one of these obstacles, when they know of its presence in a particular case.[13]

---

[12] Cappello, *De Sacramentis,* III, n. 174; Prümmer, *Manuale Theologiae Moralis,* III, n. 740; Blat, *Commentarium Textus,* III, i, 522.

[13] Canon 1018. Cfr. also, *Catechism of the Council of Trent, de matrimonii sacramento,* c. viii, n. 30.

CHAPTER XI

THE DUTIES OF PASTORS AFTER COMPLETING THE PUBLICATIONS

Canon 1029. Si alius parochus investigationem aut publicationes peregerit, de harum exitu statim per authenticum documentum certiorem reddat parochum, qui matrimonio assistere debet.

Canon 1030, § 1. Peractis investigationibus et publicationibus, parochus matrimonio ne assistat, antequam omnia documenta necessaria receperit, et praeterea, nisi rationabilis causa aliud postulet, tres dies decurrerint ab ultima publicatione.

These two canons deal principally with the coordination of the various agencies of inquiry. It is comparatively a rare case, in which the investigation can be confined to one parish, and conducted entirely by that one pastor. Generally, at least one of the parties will belong to some other parish, or will have spent a notable period of time in another place, or will have been baptized elsewhere. In any of these circumstances, the assistance of another priest or Ordinary will have to be availed of, and the prescriptions contained in canons 1029 and 1030 observed—that is, all documents and letters will have to be forwarded to the pastor who is to assist at the marriage. No matter how certain he is of the free state of the parties, that pastor may not witness the marriage, except in an emergency, until he has received the documents.[1]

ART. 1. THE RECIPIENT OF THE DOCUMENTS

Blat[2] gives to the words *parochum qui matrimonio assistere debet* in canon 1029, the same interpretation he placed on the

[1] Benedictus XIV, ep., "*Paucis abhinc,*" 19 Mart. 1758—*Coll. P. F.*, n. 410.

[2] Blat, *Commentarium Textus*, III, i, 524.

term *parochus cui jus est assistendi* in canon 1020, § 1. According to his view, the documents should be sent to one of the proper pastors; to the one of them who is to assist at the marriage, or, if none of them is actually to witness the wedding, to the one of them who has licensed,[3] or delegated[4] another priest to assist.

This interpretation may be admitted in canon 1020, § 1, because of the authority behind it there, and especially because the nature of the investigation makes it expedient that it be carried on by one who is familiar with the parties. But the same arguments cannot be applied in canon 1029.

There is no reason why the documents should not be sent to the pastor who is actually going to assist at the marriage, whether he is one of the proper pastors, or a pastor licensed to assist, according to canon 1097, § 1, 3°. It is true that the Code evidences its preference that a proper pastor witness the marriage, and that it regards any other arrangement as extraordinary. Nevertheless, the extraordinary arrangement is perfectly lawful, and assistance in such a case is put on a par with the regular assistance, since canon 1097, § 3 gives these pastors full right to the stole fees.

Therefore, the pastor who is to assist at a marriage in his own parish, in virtue of a license granted him by one of the proper pastors of the parties, can be regarded as included in the term *qui assistere debet* in canon 1029, and it is to him that the documents described in that canon should be directed. This is the interpretation generally given to this canon by authors.[5]

Sending these documents to a pastor, who, it is known, will not assist at the marriage, merely delays the immediate notification prescribed in this canon. When an impediment has been discovered, this delay involves a special risk. The important thing is to get the notice to the strategic point just as soon as possible. An interpretation which defeats the purpose of a law must necessarily be alien to the mind of the legislator.[6]

---

[3] Canon 1097, § 3.

[4] Canon 1095, § 2.

[5] Wernz-Vidal, *Jus Canonicum,* V, n. 134; Vermeersch-Creusen, *Epitome,* II, n. 289; Cerato, *Matrimonium,* p. 38.

[6] R. 88, R. J., in VI°: "Certum est quod is committit in legum, qui legis verba complectens, contra legis nititur voluntatem."

The real purpose of the term *parochum qui assistere debet* seems to be, to exclude those priests, not themselves pastors, who are to assist at a marriage in a parish by virtue of special delegation. The Code wishes to place the responsibility of receiving and reviewing the documents upon some certain definite person, and chooses the pastor of the parish in which the marriage is to be celebrated.

Art. 2. The Necessary Documents

The necessary documents mentioned in canon 1030 will vary according to the circumstances. The following is a complete list of these documents: (1) The certificates of baptism, from each party; these are required even from baptized non-Catholics. There are only two cases excepted, namely, when one party was never baptized, and the dispensation from the impediment of disparity of cult has been obtained, and secondly, when the records of baptism are in the register of the church where the marriage is to be celebrated. (2) Letters certifying that the banns were published, from the pastors of all the other parishes where the publication was obligatory. If a dispensation from the banns was obtained, this document should be forwarded to the pastor who is to assist, or at least a letter certifying that fact signed by the pastor who obtained the dispensation. (3) If the private investigation was committed to another pastor, his testimonial letter certifying that it was actually conducted. The pastor should include in the testimony of publication or investigation a statement as to whether or not an impediment was discovered, and if so, whether a dispensation from it was obtained. (4) The Bishop's permission given the pastor to assist at the marriage of a *vagus* (canon 1032); of a minor, when the parents are in ignorance of or reasonably opposed to the marriage (canon 1034); of a Catholic with one who has notoriously rejected the Faith or taken up membership in a condemned society (canon 1065); of an immigrant, even though he is not actually a *vagus*;[7] and in the case where a doubtful

---

[7] S. C. de Sacramentis, instr., 4 Jul. 1921, ad 4.—*A. A. S.*, XIII [1921], 348.

impediment exists, which the pastor was unable to solve (canon 1031, § 1, 3°). (5) The documents of dispensation from all existing impediments. (6) The document of the Papal dispensation from a marriage *ratum et non consummatum*, in case one or both of the parties was previously married, and the marriage was terminated in that way; the document should also be inspected to ascertain whether a second marriage was forbidden or not. (7) The permission of the Holy See to contract a second marriage *non obstante vetito prius dato* (as in number 6, above). (8) Proof of the death of a former spouse, or the Ordinary's permission to enter a new marriage on the presumption of that death. (9) The necessary proofs with regard to the interpellations in cases of the Pauline Privilege, according to canons 1122-3. (10) The definitive sentence of an ecclesiastical tribunal (or of the Ordinary, according to canon 1990) on the nullity of a former marriage. (11) The sentence on the nullity of a previous religious profession. (12) Documents certifying the reduction of a cleric in major Orders to the lay state, and release from the obligation of celibacy, according to canon 214, § 1. (13) The certificate of confirmation should also be presented, though this is not of strict obligation.[8] The pastor should also demand the certificate of civil license, in those States where it is required by law.

Art. 3. The Form and Content of the Documents

While a simple verbal statement from the Ordinary or the other pastor would, *per se*, suffice to convey most of the information outlined above, the Code insists that formal written evidence be given the pastor who is to assist at the marriage. All the documents in the case, then, must clearly identify the party in question, must contain the specific information required, and must be drawn up in legitimate form—that is, containing notice of the date and place of their issue, and the signature and seal of the issuing authority. The general law does not demand that

[8] Vlaming *Praelectiones Juris Matrimonii*, I, 146; De Smet, *Betrothment and Marriage*, I, 32.

the documents be first authenticated by the Ordinary,[9] but the Bishop can insist on this procedure, if he chooses.[10]

The one whose duty it is to transmit a document to the pastor witnessing the marriage, must see to it that the instrument is sent out as soon as possible. In arranging a date with the parties for the celebration of the marriage, the pastor should allow sufficient time, not only for the publication of the banns, but also for the arrival of all the necessary documents. If he observes the rule laid down in canon 1030, § 1, prescribing an interval of three days after the last publication, there will seldom be any difficulty.

In case the documents are delayed in transit, and are not at hand when the day arrives for the wedding, the pastor is bound to make special efforts to secure duplicates of them, if possible, or to consult the Ordinary. If neither of these courses is open to him, and he is certain of the freedom of the parties, he may proceed with the marriage.[11]

Art. 4. The Interval After Publication

The Code introduced a new regulation in the general law, when it prescribed that the pastor should allow three days to elapse between the last publication and the celebration of the marriage. Under the old law, this was merely recommended—except in a few dioceses where particular law had made it obligatory.

The three days are to be computed according to canon 34, § 3 —that is, the day on which the publications are completed is not itself counted. Therefore, if the banns are last proclaimed on Sunday, the marriage should not take place before Thurs-

---

[9] Wernz-Vidal, *Jus Canonicum,* V, n. 133; Rossi, *De Matrimonii Celebratione,* n. 14; Cappello, *De Sacramentis,* III, n. 180, 2; Ayrinhac, *Marriage Legislation,* p. 63. There is one exception: In transmitting the testimony of free state, in the case of emigrants described in the Instruction of the Sacred Congregation of the Sacraments, July 4, 1921, n. 3—*A. A. S.*, XIII [1921], 348, the pastor must send the documents through his diocesan Curia.

[10] As in Rome. Cfr. Fourneret, *Le Mariage Chrétien,* p. 145.

[11] Cappello, *De Sacramentis,* III, n. 180, 3; Vlaming, *Praelectiones Juris Matrimonii,* I, 147.

day.[12] The obligation to observe this regulation is not a very serious one, and any reasonable cause excuses the pastor from it.[13]

Art. 5. Repeating the Publications

Canon 1030, § 2. Si intra sex menses matrimonium contractum non fuerit, publicationes repetantur, nisi aliud loci Ordinario videatur.

If, at the end of six months the marriage has not been contracted, the banns must be repeated before the wedding can be permitted, unless the Bishop decides otherwise. The six months' period is measured from the last publication actually made, not from the one which would have been made if a dispensation had not intervened.[14] Since the beginning of the period—the *terminus a quo*—is explicitly assigned, the six months are taken as they follow on the calendar, beginning from the midnight following the last publication.[15]

The Ordinary is given wide discretionary powers in this matter. He can decide that repetition is unnecessary, and without further cause, can free the pastor of the obligation of repeating the banns. This is merely a declaration, not a dispensation. It is also within his power to order a partial repetition—for example, one publication, if the marriage is celebrated within a year of the original series of publications.[16]

Although Rossi[17] denies it, the Ordinary can, it seems, order the repetition of the banns, even within six months, if he has any suspicion against the free state of the parties. This would

---

[12] Augustine, *Commentary,* V, 69, holds to the contrary, that the first day may be counted.

[13] Cappello, *De Sacramentis,* III, n. 181; Farrugia, *De Matrimonio,* n. 68; De Smet, *Betrothment and Marriage,* I, 32; Rossi, *De Matrimonii Celebratione,* n. 21; Petrovits, *New Church Law on Marriage,* p. 60.

[14] Fanfani, *De Jure Parochorum,* p. 282; Blat, *Commentarium Textus,* III, i, 525.

[15] Canon 34, § 3, 1° and 3°.

[16] Fourneret, *Le Mariage Chrétien,* p. 116, cites the new statutes of Paris, which prescribe that one publication shall be made, if an interval of six months has elapsed.

[17] Rossi, *De Matrimonii Celebratione,* n. 23.

be just another way of exercising the discretion allowed him in this canon—*nisi aliud loci Ordinario videatur.*

The pastor does not share this right with the Ordinary, and cannot determine when the banns are to be repeated, and when omitted. He is bound to repeat them, unless the Bishop excuses him from the duty.

Cerato[18] points out that this canon does not oblige the pastor to renew his personal investigation; but even though the law does not demand this, the pastor should make an inquiry covering the intervening period, for there is always the possibility that an impediment has been incurred in the meantime.

---

[18] *Matrimonium,* p. 38.

APPENDIX

THE BANNS IN OTHER LEGISLATIONS

Art. 1. In Oriental Canon Law

From the very beginning the Eastern Church has upheld the sanctity of marriage, and insisted on the assistance of the priest at its celebration. The very first extant testimony of the Christian practice of contracting marriage before the Church may be found in the letters of St. Ignatius, the bishop of Antioch.[1] During the following centuries condemnations of secret marriage were frequently issued by ecclesiastical authority,[2] and, as in the West, the civil power also exerted its influence to curb the evil of clandestine marriage.[3] Throughout the following centuries, and in modern times, many declarations have been issued against this abuse.[4]

Although clandestinity is just as strongly condemned as in the West, the practice of publishing the banns is not universally observed, and it must be remembered that the law as proposed in the Code, does not apply to these Orientals.[5]

A few of the Oriental rites, however, have adopted regulations similar to the law in force in the West. The banns are published among the Maronites, and their canons resemble very closely the law of the Council of Trent.[6] The same can be said of the

---

[1] Letter to Polycarp, c. 5—*M. P. G.*, V, 723.

[2] Thus, the Council of Laodicea, 343 ??, c. 1—Mansi, II, 563; St. John Crysostom, in his first homily on the Gospel of St. Matthew, c. 4, referred to clandestine marriage as a thing of pagan morals. The Patriarch Nicephores of Constantinople (806-815), declared that a marriage contracted without the blessing of a priest was simply fornication.—*Thesaurus Resol. S. C. C.*, CLXVIII, 181.

[3] *Novellae Justiniani*, nn. 22, 74, 117; *Novellae Leonis*, 89.

[4] These may be found in *Echos d'Orient*, XXXII [1929], 5-18.

[5] Canon 1.

[6] Synod of Mount Libanus, 1736, part 2, c. 11—*Coll. Lac.*, II, 174.

Ruthenians.[7] Within the territory of the old Austrian Empire, the banns were published by all Orientals, owing to the strict civil law.[8] Whether this is still done or not, the writer does not know.

Art. 2. In Civil Law

Soon after the Reformation, civil authorities began to adopt this legislation. In France, there was a royal edict of 1579, which commanded the publication of the banns.[9] Later, there were other decrees of the Kings, the law in the Code Napoleon, and the revised law of 1907.[10] England retained the old practice, to a certain extent, as a custom, and then, in 1753, Lord Hardwick's Act made it law.[11]

Belgium,[12] Sweden,[13] Austria, and Germany[14] have regulations on the banns, and the Italian Concordat of 1929 makes provision for their publication.[15]

The civil marriage licenses of the American states can trace their history, through the English practice, to the dispensation, or "Bishop's license" granted in England, excusing the parties from the observance of the laws of Parliament already referred to;[16] this was, in turn, a legacy of the old canon law. The Act of 1753 was never extended to the American colonies, but the

---

[7] Prov. Synod of the Ruthenians at Zamoscia, 1720, n. viii—*Acta Synod. Ruthen.*, p. 88; S. C. de Prop. Fide, 6 Oct. 1863,—*Coll. Lac.*, II, 564.

[8] Papp-Szilágyi, *Enchiridion Juris Ecclesiae Orientalis Catholicae*, nn. 125-6.

[9] The Edict of Blois. The law, according to most of the jurists, attempted to add the penalty of invalidity to marriages celebrated without the banns. Cfr. Tourneley, *Praelectiones Theologicae*, III, 387.

[10] Rousseaud de Lacombe, *Recueil de Jurisprudence*, p. 62; Fourneret, *Le Mariage Chrétien*, p. 111.

[11] *A. E. R.*, XXXVII [1907], 123, cites several references to the banns during the seventeenth century. On the law of 1753, consult Blackstone, *Commentary*, I, 439.

[12] De Smet, *De Sponsalibus et Matrimonio* (ed. 1909), I, 48.

[13] Ringrose, *Marriage and Divorce Laws*, art. "Banns."

[14] Wernz, *Jus Decretalium*, IV, 197; Woigeck, *Das Aufgebots der Ehe*, pp. 48-54.

[15] As reproduced in the *I. E. R.*, XXXIV [1929], 509.

[16] Richmond and Hall, *Marriage and the State*, p. 17.

various colonial legislatures adopted the publications in one form or another, the New England settlements preferring the making of the announcements by civil officials at the town meeting.[17]

Gradually, the present license system replaced the publications. Licenses are now required in practically all the states. Three permit the substitution of the ecclesiastical banns for the civil license.[18]

While it is the duty of the secular authority to cooperate in discouraging sudden and clandestine marriages, it must not be inferred that the civil license or the proclaiming of the banns by civil officers can be accepted as a substitute for the publishing of the banns in the church. It has been expressly denied by the Holy See that such provisions made by the civil authorities satisfy the requirements of the canon law,[19] and the reasons for this are quite clear. The Church wishes all things pertaining to the rite of marriage to be under the supervision of Her ministers. Moreover, a declaration by the secular authorities that they found no impediments to the marriage according to the civil law, would not certify the absence of all impediments recognized by the Church.

---

[17] Howard, *History of Matrimonial Institutions,* II, 131-45; 285-300; 401-445.

[18] They are Ohio, Maryland, and Georgia. Cfr. May, *Marriage Laws in the U. S.*, p. 333.

[19] S. C. S. Off. (Vic. Ap. Jamaicae), 12 Jan. 1881—*Coll. P. F.*, n. 1545.

BIBLIOGRAPHY

Sources

Acta Apostolicae Sedis, (*A.A.S.*), (Rome, 1909—).

Acta Sanctae Sedis, (*A.S.*), (41 vols., Rome, 1865-1908).

Bullarium Diplomatum et Privilegiorum Sanctorum Romanorum Pontificum, Taurinensis editio . . . auspicante Cardinali Francisco Gaude, (24 vols., Turin, 1857-1872).

Bullarii Romani Continuatio Summorum Pontificum, (19 vols., Prato, 1756-1883).

Codex Juris Canonici Pii X Pontificis Maximi jussu digestus Benedicti Papae XV auctoritate promulgatus, (Rome, 1917).

Codicis Juris Canonici Fontes cura Emi. Petri Gasparri editi, (5 vols., Rome: Typis Polyg., 1923-1929).

Collectanea Sacrae Congregationis de Propaganda Fide, (2 vols., Rome, 1907).

Collectio Lacensis, Acta et Decreta Conciliorum Recentiorum, (7 vols., Freiburg in Breisgau, 1870-1879).

Concilium Plenarium Totius Americae Septentrionalis Baltimori Habitum anno 1852, (Baltimore, 1853).

Concilii Plenarii Baltimorensis II Acta et Decreta, (2. ed., Baltimore, 1894).

Corpus Juris Canonici, editio Lipsiensis II (Richter-Friedberg), (2 vols., Leipzig: Welter, 1922).

Corpus Juris Civilis, (Krueger-Mommsen-Schoell-Kroell), (5. ed., 3 vols., Berlin: Weidmann, 1928).

Harduinus, *Acta Conciliorum*, (12 vols., Paris, 1715).

Hartzheim, *Concilia Germaniae*, (11 vols., Cologne, 1715-1790).

Mansi, *Sacrorum Conciliorum Nova et Amplissima Collectio*, (59 vols., Leipzig: Welter, 1901-1927).

Monumenta Germaniae Historica, Leges, (5 vols., Leipzig: Hiersemann, 1925).

Pallottini, *Collectio Omnium Conclusionum et Resolutionum apud Sacram Congregationem Cardinalium Sacri Concilii Tridentini Interpretum*, (17 vols., Rome, 1886).

Thesaurus Resolutionum Sacrae Congregationis Concilii, (168 vols., Rome, 1745-1908).

Zamboni, *Collectio Declarationum Sacrae Congregationis Cardinalium Sacri Concilii Tridentini Interpretum*, (5 vols., Arras, 1861).

Reference Works

Aertnys, J.,—Damen, C. A., *Theologia Moralis*, (3. ed., 2 vols., Turin: Marietti, 1928).

Alphonsus de Ligorio, St., *Theologia Moralis,* (2 vols., Turin, 1888).

Augustinus, Antonius, *Antiquae Colleciones Decretalium,* (Lerida, 1576).

Ayrinhac, H. A., *Marriage Legislation in the New Code of Canon Law,* (New York: Benziger, 1918).

[Bachofen], Charles Augustine, *Commentary on the New Code of Canon Law,* (8 vols., St. Louis: Herder, 1919-1923).

Ballerini, A.,—Palmieri, D., *Opus Theologicum Morale,* (2. ed., 8 vols., Prato, 1892).

Bangen, Joannes H., *Instructio Practica de Sponsalibus et Matrimonio,* (2 vols., Münster, 1853).

Barbosa, Augustinus, *De Officio et Potestate Episcopi,* (2 vols., Lyons, 1656).

Barbosa, Augustinus, *Collectanea Doctorum tam Veterum quam Recentiorum in Jus Pontificium Universum,* (6 vols., Lyons, 1669).

Baronius, Caesarius Cardinal, *Annales Ecclesiastici,* (37 vols., Bari, 1864-1883).

Bernardus Papiensis, *Summa Decretalium* (Laspeyres ed.), (Ratisbon, 1860).

Bingham, Joseph, *The Antiquities of the Christian Church,* (2. ed., 2 vols., London, 1856).

Blat, Albertus, *Commentarium Textus Codicis Juris Canonici,* (5 vols., Rome: Typog. Institut. Pii IX, 1920-1927).

Bouix, D., *Tractatus de Judiciis Ecclesiasticis,* (3. ed., 2 vols., Paris, 1884).

Buckland, W. W., *A Text Book of Roman Law,* (Cambridge: Cambridge Univ. Press, 1921).

Cappello, F., *Tractatus Canonico Moralis de Sacramentis,* (2. ed., 3 vols., Rome: Marietti, 1927).

Carriere, J., *Praelectiones Theologicae,* (3 vols., Paris, 1837).

Cerato, Prosdocimus, *Matrimonium a Codice Juris Canonici Desumptum,* (4. ed., Padua: Typis Seminar., 1929).

Chelodi, Joannes, *Jus Matrimoniale juxta Codicem Juris Canonici,* (3. ed., Trent: Libr. Edit. Trident., 1921).

Corradus, Pyrrhus, *Praxis Dispensationum Apostolicarum Pro Utroque Foro,* (5. ed., Cologne, 1697).

Cosci, Christophorus, *De Sponsalibus Vota Decisiva,* (Rome, 1763).

Costello, John, *Domicile and Quasi-Domicile,* (Washington: Cath. Univ., 1930).

Cuq, Edouard, *Les Institutions Juridiques des Romains,* (Paris, 1891).

D'Annibale, Joseph Cardinal, *Summa Theologiae Moralis,* (3. ed., 3 vols., Rome, 1892).

De Becker, Julius, *Praelectiones Canonicae,* (2. ed., Louvain, 1903).

Deshayes, F., *Questions Pratiques de Droit Canonique sur le Mariage,* (Paris, 1898).

De Smet, A., *Betrothment and Marriage,* (2 vols., St. Louis: Herder, 1912).

De Smet, A., *Betrothment and Marriage,* (2. ed., 2 vols., St. Louis: Herder, 1923).

Devoti, Joannes, *Institutionum Canonicarum Libri Quatuor*, (5. ed., 2 vols., Liege, 1883).

Engel, Ludovicus, *Collegium Universi Juris Canonici*, (Benevento, 1760).

Esmein, A., *Le Mariage en Droit Canonique*, (2 vols., Paris, 1891).

Esmein, A., *Le Mariage en Droit Canonique*, (2. ed., vol. i, Paris: Sirey, 1929).

Fagnanus, Prosperus, *Commentarium in Quartum Librum Decretalium*, (Venice, 1696).

Fanfani, Ludovicus, *De Jure Parochorum ad Normam Codicis Juris Canonici*, (Turin: Marietti, 1924).

Feíje, Henricus, *De Impedimentis et Dispensationibus Matrimonii*, (2 vols., Louvain, 1885).

Ferraris, Lucius, *Prompta Bibliotheca Canonica, Juridica, Moralis Theologica, et Liturgica*, (8 vols., Rome, 1889).

Ferreres, Joannes, *Compendium Theologiae Moralis*, (8 ed., 2 vols., Barcelona: Subirana, 1918).

Ferry, William, *Stole Fees*, (Washington: Cath. Univ., 1930).

Fourneret, Pierre, *Le Mariage Chrétien*, (Paris: Beauchesne, 1925).

Freisen, Joseph, *Geschichte des Canonischen Eherechts*, (Paderborn, 1893).

Gally, H., *Considerations on Clandestine Marriage*, (2. ed., London, 1750).

Gasparri, Petrus Cardinal, *Tractatus Canonicus de Matrimonio*, (2 vols., Paris, 1891).

Giraldi, Ubaldus, *Expositio Juris Pontificii*, (2 vols., Rome, 1830).

Gonzalez, Emmanuel . . . Tellez, *Commentaria Perpetua in Singulos Textus Quinque Librorum Decretalium Gregorii IX*, (5 vols., Venice, 1758).

Grandclaude, E., *Jus Canonicum*, (3 vols., Paris, 1883).

Gutierrez, Joannes, *Liber Tertius Canonicarum Questionum*, (3 vols., Norberg, 1647).

Hefele, Carl Joseph von, *Conciliengeschicte*, (2. ed., 9 vols., Freiburg in Breisgau, 1875-1890).

Hostiensis, (Henricus de Segusio), *Commentaria in Quartum Librum Decretalium*, (Venice, 1581).

Hostiensis, *Summa Aurea*, (Venice, 1570).

Howard, George E., *History of Matrimonial Institutions*, (3 vols., Chicago, 1904).

Joder, J., *Formulaire Matrimonial*, (3. ed., Paris, 1891).

Kenrick, Franciscus, *Theologia Moralis*, (2 vols., Mechlin, 1861).

Knecht, August, *Handbuch des Katholischen Eherechts auf grund des Codex Juris Canonici*, (Freiburg in Breisgau: Herder, 1928).

Könings, A., *Theologia Moralis*, (2 vols., Boston, 1889).

Leage, R. W., *Roman Private Law*, (3. ed., London: Macmillan, 1920).

Lehmkuhl, Augustinus, *Theologia Moralis*, (12. ed., 2 vols., Freiburg in Breisgau: Herder, 1914).

Martene, Edmundus, *De Antiquis Ecclesiae Ritibus*, (4 vols., Rouen, 1700).

Mascardus, Joseph, *Conclusiones Probationum Omnium*, (3 vols., Venice, 1593).

May, Geoffrey, *Marriage Laws and Decisions in the United States*, (New York: Russell Sage Foundation, 1929).

Mazzaeus, Franciscus, *De Matrimonio Conscientiae*, (Rome, 1766).

Menochius, Jacobus, *De Arbitrariis Judicum Quaestiones et Causae*, (Venice, 1569).

Menochius, Jacobus, *De Praesumptionibus, Conjecturis, Signis, et Indiciis Commentaria*, (Cologne, 1686).

Migne, J., *Patrologiae Cursus Completus, series latina*, (221 vols., Paris, 1844-1855).

Noldin, H., *Summa Theologiae Moralis*, (16. ed., 3 vols., Innsbruck: Rauch, 1923).

Ojetti, Benedictus, *Synopsis Rerum Moralium et Juris Pontificii*, (3. ed., 3 vols., Rome: Univ. Greg., 1909-1914).

O'Neill, William, *Papal Rescripts of Favor*, (Washington: Cath. Univ., 1930).

Panormitanus, (Nicholas de Tudeschio), *Commentaria*, (8 vols., Venice, 1588).

Papp-Szilágyi, Joseph, *Enchiridion Juris Ecclesiae Orientalis Catholicae*, (2. ed., Nagyvárad, 1880).

Pignatelli, Jacobus, *Consultationes Canonicae*, (11 vols., Cologne, 1700).

Pirhing, Ernricus, *Jus Canonicum Nova Methodo Explicatum*, (4 vols., Dillinger, 1722).

Pontius, Basilius, *Tractatus de Sacramento Matrimonii*, (Brussels, 1627).

Prümmer, Dominicus, *Manuale Theologiae Moralis*, (3. ed., 3 vols., Freiburg in Breisgau: Herder, 1923).

Raymond of Pennafort, *Summa*, (Verona, 1744).

Reiffenstuel, Anacletus, *Jus Canonicum Universum*, (4 vols., Antwerp, 1743).

Richmond, M., and Hall, F., *Marriage and the State*, (New York: Russell Sage Foundation, 1929).

Ringrose, Hyacinthe, *Marriage and Divorce Laws*, (New York: Musson Draper, 1911).

Rittershutius, Cunradus, *Expositio Methodica Novellarum Imperatoris Justiniani*, (2. ed., Florence, 1839).

Rossi, Joseph, *De Matrimonii Celebratione juxta Codicem Juris Canonici*, (Rome: Pustet, 1924).

Rufinus, *Summa Decretorum*, (Paderborn, 1902).

Sanchez, Thomas, *Disputationum de Sancto Matrimonii Sacramento Libri Sex*, (3 vols., Geneva, 1602).

Santi, Franciscus, *Praelectiones Juris Canonicae*, (5 vols., Ratisbon, 1892).

Scavini, Petrus, *Theologia Moralis Universa*, (2. ed., 2 vols., Paris, 1867).

Schenk, Francis, *The Matrimonial Impediments of Mixed Religion and Disparity of Cult*, (Washington: Cath. Univ., 1929).

Scherer, Rudolph von, *Handbuch des Kirchenrechts*, (2 vols., Gran, 1898).

Schmalzgrueber, Franciscus, *Jus Ecclesiasticum*, (12 vols., Rome, 1844).

Smith, William, *Dictionary of Greek and Roman Antiquities*, (3. ed., 2 vols., London, 1891).

Soto, Dominicus, *Commentariorum in Librum Quartum Sententiarum Tomus Primus et Secundus,* (2 vols., Venice, 1569).

Stephanus, Matthias, *Commentarius in Novellas Justiniani Imperatoris,* (Florence, 1843).

Suarez, Franciscus, *Opera Omnia,* (26 vols., Paris, 1858-1861).

Tanquerey, A., *Synopsis Theologiae Moralis et Pastoralis,* (10. ed., 3 vols., Rome: Desclée, 1925).

Tourneley, Honoratus, *Praelectiones Theologicae,* (Paris, 1743).

Ubach, Joseph, *Compendium Theologiae Moralis,* (2 vols., Freiburg in Breisgau: Herder, 1927).

Van Hove, A., *De Legibus Ecclesiasticis,* (Mechlin: Dessain, 1930).

Vecchiotti, Septimus, *Institutiones Canonicae,* (19. ed., 3 vols., Turin, 1886).

Vermeersch, A., *De Forma Sponsalium et Matrimonii post Decretum Ne Temere,* (Bruges, 1908).

Vermeersch, A., *Theologial Moralis Principia, Responsa, Consilia,* (2. ed., 3 vols., Rome: Univ. Greg., 1926-1928).

Vermeersch, A.,—Creusen, J., *Epitome Juris Canonici,* (3. ed., 3 vols., Mechlin: Dessain, 1927).

Vlaming, T., *Praelectiones Juris Matrimonii,* (3. ed., 2 vols., Bussum: Edit. Anon., 1919).

Wernz, Franciscus, *Jus Decretalium,* (2. ed., 6 vols., Prato: Giachetti, 1911-1913).

Wernz, F.,—Vidal, P., *Jus Canonicum,* (2. ed., vols. ii, v, and vi, Rome: Univ. Greg., 1927-1928).

Woigeck, Hans, *Das Aufgebot der Ehe in seiner Geschichtlichen Entwicklung,* (Frankfort on Main, 1914).

Zitelli, Zephrinus, *Apparatus Juris Ecclesiastici,* (Rome, 1886).

Periodicals

American Ecclesiastical Review, The, (*A.E.R.*), (Philadelphia, 1889—).

Analecta Ecclesiastica, (19 vols., Rome, 1893-1911).

Apollinaris, (Rome, 1928—).

Archiv für Katholisches Kirchenrecht, (*A.k. KR.*), (Mainz, 1857—).

Canoniste Contemporain, Le, (Paris, 1878—).

Echos d'Orient, (Paris, 1897—).

Ephemerides Theologicae Lovanienses, (Louvain, 1924—).

Irish Ecclesiastical Record, The, (*I.E.R.*), (Dublin, 1865—).

Jus Pontificium, (Rome, 1921—).

Nouvelle Revue Théologique, (*N.R.T.*), (Paris, 1856—).

Theologisch-Praktische Quartalschrift, (*L.QS.*), (Linz, 1832—).

Universitas Catholica Americae

WASHINGTONII, D. C.

FACULTAS JURIS CANONICI

1931

No. 64

DEUS LUX MEA

TITULI

QUOS

AD DOCTORATUS GRADUM

IN

JURE CANONICO

APUD UNIVERSITATEM CATHOLICAM AMERICAE

CONSEQUENDUM

PUBLICE PROPUGNABIT

JACOBUS BRENDAN ROBERTS

SACERDOS ARCHIDIOECESIS

NEO-EBORACENSIS

JURIS CANONICI LICENTIATUS

HORA IX A.M., DIE XXVII MAII MCMXXXI

TITULI

IN IURE CANONICO

I.	De Dissertatione.	
II.	De Historia Iuris Canonici.	
III.	Canones 1-7	De Ambitu Codicis.
IV.	Canones 8-24	De Legibus Ecclesiasticis.
V.	Canones 25-30	De Consuetudine.
VI.	Canones 31-35	De Temporis Supputatione.
VII.	Canones 36-62	De Rescriptis.
VIII.	Canones 63-79	De Privilegiis.
IX.	Canones 80-86	De Dispensationibus.
X.	Canones 87-107	Generales Notiones de Personis.
XI.	Canones 111-117	De Clericorum Adscriptione Alicui Dioecesi.
XII.	Canones 118-123	De Iuribus et Privilegiis Clericorum.
XIII.	Canones 124-144	De Obligationibus Clericorum.
XIV.	Canones 145-195	De Officiis Ecclesiasticis.
XV.	Canones 196-210	De Potestate Ordinaria et Delegata.
XVI.	Canones 487-498	De Notione Religionis, et de Erectione et Suppressione Religionis, Provinciae, Domus.
XVII.	Canones 499-537	De Religionum Regimine.
XVIII.	Canones 538-586	De Admissione in Religionem.
XIX.	Canones 673-681	De Societatibus sive Virorum sive Mulierum in Communi Viventium sine Votis.
XX.	Canones 1012-1018	De Matrimonio in Genere.
XXI.	Canones 1019-1034	De Iis quae Matrimonii Celebrationi Praemitti debent.
XXII.	Canones 1035-1057	De Impedimentis in Genere.
XXIII.	Canones 1058-1066	De Impedimentis Impedientibus.
XXIV.	Canones 1067-1080	De Impedimentis Dirimentibus.
XXV.	Canones 1081-1093	De Consensu Matrimoniali.
XXVI.	Canones 1552-1568	De Notione Iudicii et de Foro Competenti.
XXVII.	Canones 1569-1607	De Variis Tribunalium Gradibus et Speciebus.
XXVIII.	Canones 1608-1645	De Disciplina in Tribunalibus Servanda.

XXIX.	Canones 1646-1666	De Partibus in Causa.
XXX.	Canones 1667-1705	De Actionibus et Exceptionibus.
XXXI.	Canones 1706-1725	De Causae Introductione.
XXXII.	Canones 1726-1746	De Litis Contestatione, de Litis Instantia, et de Interrogationibus Partibus in Iudicio Faciendis.
XXXIII.	Canones 1747-1836	De Probationibus.
XXXIV.	Canones 1837-1857	De Causis Incidentibus.
XXXV.	Canones 1858-1877	De Processus Publicatione, de Conclusione in Causa, de Causae Discussione, et de Sententia.
XXXVI.	Canones 1879-1891	De Appellatione.
XXXVII.	Canones 1902-1907	De Re Iudicata et de Restitutione in Integrum.
XXXVIII.	Canones 1960-1992	De Causis Matrimonialibus.
XXXIX.	Canones 2195-2198	De Natura Delicti eiusque Divisione.
XL.	Canones 2199-2211	De Imputabilitate Delicti, de Causis illam Aggravantibus vel Minuentibus, et de Iuridicis Delicti Effectibus.
XLI.	Canones 2212-2213	De Conatu Delicti.
XLII.	Canones 2214-2240	De Poenis in Genere.
XLIII.	Canones 2241-2285	De Poenis Medicinalibus seu de Censuris.
XLIV.	Canones 2286-2305	De Poenis Vindicativis.
XLV.	Canones 2306-2313	De Remediis Poenalibus et Poenitentiis.

IN IURE ROMANO

XLVI. The Periods of Roman Law.
XLVII. The Sources of Roman Law.
XLVIII. Personality.
XLIX. Slavery.
L. Citizenship.
LI. Patria Potestas.
LII. Personae in Manu.
LIII. Tutela et Cura.
LIV. Personae in Mancipio.
LV. Ownership.
LVI. De Obligationibus in Genere.
LVII. De Obligationibus Extra-Contractualibus.
LVIII. Furtum.
LIX. Damnum Injuria Datum.
LX. Injuria.

Vidit Facultas:

VALENTINUS T. SCHAAF, O.F.M., J.C.D., Vice-Decanus.

LUDOVICUS H. MOTRY, S.T.D., J.C.D., a Secretis.

FRANCISCUS J. LARDONE, S.T.D., J.U.D.

Vidit Rector Magnificus Universitatis:

JACOBUS HUGO RYAN, S.T.D., Ph.D., LL.D., Litt.D.

VITA

James Brendan Roberts was born on February 3, 1906, in New York City. He received his elementary education in Resurrection School, and his high school, and college training in Cathedral College, New York City. In September, 1923, he entered St. Joseph's Seminary, Dunwoodie, New York, and was ordained priest on May 25, 1929. In October of that year, he entered the School of Canon Law at the Catholic University of America, in Washington, D. C.

CATHOLIC UNIVERSITY OF AMERICA

CANON LAW STUDIES

1. Freriks, Rev. Celestine A., C.PP.S., J.C.D., Religious Congregations in Their External Relations, 121 pp., 1916.
2. Galliher, Rev. Daniel M., O.P., J.C.D., Canonical Elections, 117 pp., 1917.
3. Borkowski, Rev. Aurelius L., O.F.M., J.C.D., De Confraternitatibus Ecclesiasticis, 136 pp., 1918.
4. Castillo, Rev. Cayo, J.C.D., Disertacion Historico-canonica sobre la Potestad del Cabildo en Sede Vacante o Impedida del Vicario Capitular, 99 pp., 1919 (1918).
5. Kubelbeck, Rev. William J., S.T.B., J.C.D., The Sacred Penitentiaria and Its Relations to Faculties of Ordinaries and Priests, 129 pp., 1918.
6. Petrovits, Rev. Joseph J. C., S.T.D., J.C.D., The New Church Law on Matrimony, X-461 pp., 1919.
7. Hickey, Rev. John J., S.T.B., J.C.D., Irregularities and Simple Impediments in the New Code of Canon Law, 100 pp., 1920.
8. Klekotka, Rev. Peter J., S.T.B., J.C.D., Diocesan Consultors, 179 pp., 1920.
9. Wannenmacher, Rev. Francis, J.C.D., The Evidence in Ecclesiastical Procedure Affecting the Marriage Bond, 1920. (Not Printed.)
10. Golden, Rev. Henry Francis, J.C.D., Parochial Benefices in the New Code, IV-119 pp., 1921. (Printed 1925.)
11. Koudelka, Rev. Charles J., J.C.D., Pastors, Their Rights and Duties According to the New Code of Canon Law, 211 pp., 1921.
12. Melo, Rev. Antonius, O.F.M., J.C.D., De Exemptione Regularium, X-188 pp., 1921.
13. Schaaf, Rev. Valentine Theodore, O.F.M., S.T.B., J.C.D., The Cloister, X-180 pp., 1921.
14. Burke, Rev. Thomas Joseph, S.T.B., J.C.D., Competence in Ecclesiastical Tribunals, IV-117 pp., 1922.
15. Leech, Rev. George Leo, J.C.D., A Comparative Study of the Constitution "Apostolicae Sedis" and the "Codex Juris Canonici," 179 pp., 1922.
16. Motry, Rev. Hubert Louis, S.T.D., J.C.D., Diocesan Faculties according to the Code of Canon Law, II-167 pp., 1922.
17. Murphy, Rev. George Lawrence, J.C.D., Delinquencies and Penalties in the Administration and the Reception of the Sacraments, IV-121 pp., 1923.

18. O'Reilly, Rev. John Anthony, S.T.B., J.C.D., Ecclesiastical Sepulture in the New Code of Canon Law, II-129 pp., 1923.
19. Michalicka, Rev. Wenceslas Cyrill, O.S.B., J.C.D., Judicial Procedure in Dismissal of Clerical Exempt Religious, 107 pp., 1923.
20. Dargin, Rev. Edward Vincent, S.T.B., J.C.D., Reserved Cases According to the Code of Canon Law, IV-103 pp., 1924.
21. Godfrey, Rev. John A., S.T.B., J.C.D., The Right of Patronage According to the Code of Canon Law, 153 pp., 1924.
22. Hagedorn, Rev. Francis Edward, J.C.D., General Legislation on Indulgences, II-154 pp., 1924.
23. King, Rev. James Ignatius, J.C.D., The Administration of the Sacraments to Dying Non-Catholics, V-141 pp., 1924.
24. Winslow, Rev. Francis Joseph, A.F.M., J.C.D., Vicars and Prefects Apostolic, IV-149 pp., 1924.
25. Correa, Rev. Jose Servelion, S.T.L., J.C.D., La Potestad Legislativa de la Iglesia Catolica, IV-127 pp., 1925.
26. Dugan, Rev. Henry Francis, M.A., J.C.D., The Judiciary Department of the Diocesan Curia, 87 pp., 1925.
27. Keller, Rev. Charles Frederick, S.T.B., J.C.D., Mass Stipends, 167 pp., 1925.
28. Paschang, Rev. John Linus, J.C.D., The Sacramentals According to the Code of Canon Law, 129 pp., 1925.
29. Piontek, Rev. Cyrillus, O.F.M., S.T.B., J.C.D., De Indulto Exclaustrationis necnon Saecularizationis, XIII-289 pp., 1925.
30. Kearney, Rev. Richard Joseph, S.T.B., J.C.D., Sponsors at Baptism According to the Code of Canon Law, IV-127 pp., 1925.
31. Bartlett, Rev. Chester Joseph, A.M., LL.B., J.C.D., The Tenure of Parochial Property in the United States of America, V-108 pp., 1926.
32. Kilker, Rev. Adrian Jerome, J.C.D., Extreme Unction, V-425 pp., 1926.
33. McCormick, Rev. Robert Emmett, J.C.D., Confessors of Religious, VIII-266 pp., 1926.
34. Miller, Rev. Newton Thomas, J.C.D., Founded Masses According to the Code of Canon Law, VII-93 pp., 1926.
35. Roelker, Rev. Edward G., S.T.D., J.C.D., Principles of Privilege According to the Code of Canon Law, XI-166 pp., 1926.
36. Bakalarczyk, Rev. Richardus, M.I.C., J.U.D., De Novitiatu, VIII-208 pp., 1927.
37. Pizzuti, Rev. Lawrence, O.F.M., J.U.L., De Parochis Religiosis, 1927. (Not Printed.)
38. Bliley, Rev. Nicholas Martin, O.S.B., J.C.D., Altars According to the Code of Canon Law, XIX-132 pp., 1927.
39. Brown, Brendan Francis, A.B., LL.M., J.U.D., The Canonical Juristic Personality with Special Reference to its Status in the United States of America, V-212 pp., 1927.

40. CAVANAUGH, REV. WILLIAM THOMAS, C.P., J.U.D., The Reservation of the Blessed Sacrament, VIII-101 pp., 1927.

41. DOHENY, REV. WILLIAM J., C.S.C., A.B., J.U.D., Church Property: Modes of Acquisition, X-118 pp., 1927.

42. FELDHAUS, REV. ALOYSIUS H., C.PP.S., J.C.D., Oratories, IX-141 pp., 1927.

43. KELLY, REV. JAMES PATRICK, A.B., J.C.D., The Jurisdiction of the Simple Confessor, X-208 pp., 1927.

44. NEUBERGER, REV. NICHOLAS J., J.C.D., Canon 6 or the Relation of the Codex Juris Canonici to the Preceding Legislation, V-95 pp., 1927.

45. O'KEEFFE, REV. GERALD MICHAEL, J.C.D., Matrimonial Dispensations, Powers of Bishops, Priests, and Confessors, VIII-232 pp., 1927.

46. QUIGLEY, REV. JOSEPH, A.M., A.B., J.C.D., Condemned Societies, 139 pp., 1927.

47. ZAPLOTNIK, REV. IOANNES LEO, J.C.D., De Vicariis Foraneis, X-142, 1927.

48. DUSKIE, REV. JOHN ALOYSIUS, A.B., J.C.D., The Canonical Status of the Orientals in the United States, VIII-196 pp., 1928.

49. HYLAND, REV. FRANCIS EDWARD, J.C.D., Excommunication, Its Nature, Historical Development and Effects, VIII-181 pp., 1928.

50. REINMANN, REV. GERALD JOSEPH, O.M.C., J.C.D., The Third Order Secular of Saint Francis, 201 pp., 1928.

51. SCHENK, REV. FRANCIS J., J.C.D., The Matrimonial Impediments of Mixed Religion and Disparity of Cult. XVI-318 pp., 1929.

52. COADY, REV. JOHN JOSEPH, S.T.D., J.U.D., A.M., The Appointment of Pastors, VIII-150 pp., 1929.

53. KAY, REV. THOMAS HENRY, J.C.D., Competence in Matrimonial Procedure, VIII-164 pp., 1929.

54. TURNER, REV. SIDNEY JOSEPH, C.P., J.U.D., The Vow of Poverty, XLIX-217 pp., 1929.

55. KEARNEY, REV. RAYMOND A., A.B., S.T.D., J.C.D., The Principles of Delegation, VII-149 pp., 1929.

56. CONRAN, REV. EDWARD JAMES, A.B., J.C.D., The Interdict, V-163 pp., 1930.

57. O'NEILL, REV. WILLIAM H., J.C.D., Papal Rescripts of Favor, VII-219 pp., 1930.

58. BASTNAGEL, REV. CLEMENT VINCENT, J.U.D., The Appointment of Parochial Adjutants and Assistants, XV-262 pp., 1930.

59. FERRY, REV. WILLIAM A., A.B., J.C.D., Stole Fees, X-108 pp., 1930.

60. COSTELLO, REV. JOHN MICHAEL, A.B., J.C.D., Domicile and Quasi-Domicile, VII-201 pp., 1930.

61. KREMER, REV. MICHAEL NICHOLAS, A.B., S.T.B., J.C.D., Church Support in the United States, VI-137 pp., 1930.

62. ANGULO, REV. LUIS, C.M., J.C.L., Legislación de la Iglesia Católica sobre la intención en la aplicación de la Misa, 1931.

63. Frey, Rev. Wolfgang, O.S.B., A.B., J.C.L., The Act of Religious Profession, 1931.
64. Roberts, Rev. James Brendan, A.B., J.C.L., The Banns of Marriage, 1931.
65. Ryder, Rev. Raymond Aloysius, A.B., J.C.L., Simony, 1931.
66. Campagna, Rev. Michael Angelo, Ph.B., J.U.L., Il Vicario Generale del Vescovo, 1931.
67. Cox, Rev. Joseph Godfrey, A.B., J.C.L., The Administration of Seminaries, 1931.
68. Gregory, Rev. Donald Joseph, S.T.B., J.U.L., The Pauline Privelege, 1931.
69. Donohue, Rev. John Francis, A.M., J.C.L., The Impediment of Crime, 1931.
70. Dooley, Rev. Eugene A., O.M.I., A.B., J.C.L., Church Law on Sacred Relics, 1931.

www.ingramcontent.com/pod-product-compliance
Lightning Source LLC
LaVergne TN
LVHW050216080826
844660LV00012B/421

9780813222530